How to Use This Book

This book has many ways to help you easily find the information you need:

- **Brief Contents:** This is the table of contents for the book, listing only the sections and chapter titles. Each section of the book begins with a more complete list of its contents.
- **Question and Correct:** This is a list of typical questions writers ask. When you find a question similar to the one you have, you'll see the section number and page to turn to. You won't need to know any terminology.
- **Sections of the Book:** Here you'll find summaries of the contents of each part of the book to help you find the type of information you need.
- **HINT Boxes:** Throughout the book you'll find HINT boxes that offer advice, help you remember rules, and keep you from making mistakes that often arise.
- **Questions at the Beginning of Each Part of the Book:** To help you find what you need in a section of the book, you'll find a list of more questions writers typically ask.
- **Glossary of Usage:** This is an alphabetical list of words that can be confusing, such as when to write "may" and when to write "can" (or "your" or "you're") or whether or not terms such as "could of" or "use to" are correct.
- **Glossary of Grammatical Terms:** This is an alphabetical list of grammatical terms and their definitions.
- **Index:** This is an alphabetical list of the topics covered in this book with the pages to turn to, to find explanations.
- **Correction Symbols:** This is a list of correction symbols many instructors use when reading student papers.

Sections of the Book

I   Writing and Speaking

Here you'll find checklists for planning, writing, and
revising papers and information about developing a thesis
statement, linking sentences and paragraphs, writing
introductions and conclusions, and using computers
effectively when you write. There is also information and
advice on developing oral and multimedia presentations.

II   Sentence Choices

Included here is information about composing
sentences, including how to write clear, effective
sentences that don't overuse the passive voice and are
varied, concise, and nonsexist in word choices. You'll
also find help with using transitions that connect
sentences and paragraphs smoothly.

III   Sentence Grammar

This section explains the rules of grammar and includes
many HINT boxes to help you avoid such errors as
fragments, comma splices and fused sentences, subject-
verb agreement errors, pronoun and adjective errors,
dangling modifiers, and shifts in voice and number.

IV   Punctuation

This section begins with an overview of sentence
punctuation patterns, and then you'll find information
on using commas, apostrophes, semicolons, quotation
marks, and other punctuation.

V   Mechanics

Here you'll find information when you need to check on
which words to capitalize, when to use italics, how to
write out numbers and when to use figures instead,
which words can be abbreviated and how to do that,
and what rules you can use for spelling correctly.

VI   Multilingual Speakers (ESL)

For students whose first language is not English this
section includes a discussion of the American style of
writing and a list of resources for learning English.
There are also explanations of English verbs, count and
noncount nouns, articles, prepositions, words that
should not be repeated or omitted, and idioms.

VII Research

Here you'll find extensive help with moving through the process of planning, researching, writing, and revising research papers. There is also advice and information about using libraries; going online to find, evaluate, and document information; using search engines; avoiding plagiarism; and designing effective documents (by preparing papers appropriately and by using visuals).

The "Research" section offers advice on choosing a topic and integrating sources into your paper. This section will also help you use search engines efficiently, locate useful resources, find Web addresses to lead you to useful starting places, and follow guidelines for document design.

VIII Documentation

This section includes information on how to document sources in MLA, APA, *Chicago Manual of Style* (CM), and Council of Science Editors (CSE) style. There is also an extensive list of style manuals in various fields and sources for writing in various fields.

I hope that you find this book easy to use and that it becomes a writing friend to keep nearby as you write. Then you'll be more confident that you are writing correctly and effectively and are conveying your ideas in ways that others will appreciate and respect.

Muriel Harris

Question and Correct

Research   p. 121

- How do I start a library search
  for information?   36b
- How do I start searching the Internet
  for information?   36c
- What are some useful Web sites to try?   36d
- How do I know if a source is reliable?   37
- When do I cite a source?   38e
- How do I set margins and spacing on papers? 39a
- How and when should I use tables and charts? 39b

More questions about research: pp. 121–123

Documentation   p. 173

- What is MLA style?   40
- Is there a list of which examples are given for
  MLA style?   40c
- What are some ways that APA and MLA are
  alike and different?   41
- Is there a list of which examples are given for
  APA style?   41c
- How do I set up my paper (title, margins, etc.)
  –in MLA format?   40d
  –in APA format?   41d
- What are some other style manuals and
  sources for other fields?   44

**More questions about how to document
sources:**   pp. 173–175

Glossary of Usage   p. 255

- What is the difference between "accept"
  and "except"?   USAGE
- Is it acceptable to write "a lot" or "and etc."? USAGE
- What's the difference between similar words
  such as "anyone" and "any one," "awful"
  and "awfully"?   USAGE
- When do I use "that" or "which" and "who"
  or "whom"?   USAGE

Glossary of Grammatical Terms   p. 266

I
Writing and Speaking

Contents of this section

QUESTION & CORRECT

	SECTION	PAGE
✦ When I start planning or when I'm drafting my paper, what questions should I ask myself?	1a	3
✦ What are HOCs (Higher Order Concerns), and why are they important?	1a	3
✦ Why is thinking about the purpose and audience important?	1a	3

1

Checklist for Effective Papers/Presentations

1a   HOCs (Higher Order Concerns)

Listed here are the Higher Order Concerns (HOCs) that help to make your writing effective:

Purpose

Be sure your purpose fits the assignment. If you are asked to persuade your readers, that is different than writing to explain or summarize. If you are asked to describe, your purpose is to help your readers envision your subject. Read the assignment carefully, and note the verbs carefully. Are you asked to **compare** two or more things? **Analyze? Describe? Explain? Persuade? State** your opinion?

You can clarify your purpose by answering the questions, "Why am I writing this? What am I trying to accomplish?" For example, do you want your readers to take some action? Accept your view? Understand something they didn't know before? Share some experience of yours?

Audience

Think about your readers. Check to see that they are the appropriate audience for your assignment and purpose. Think about what they already know and what they most likely want to know or don't need to know. Should you add any information or background summary to help them understand your topic?

If you are arguing or persuading, are you writing to those who are likely to disagree? If so, how can you convince them? Is there some common ground, some aspects of the argument you share with them, that will help in getting those who disagree to consider what you are writing?

Thesis statement

Your thesis is the main idea or subject of the paper, and it is often the answer to a question you have posed to yourself. You should be able to summarize the thesis briefly in a sentence or two, and your paper should state it clearly. Think of the thesis as a promise that you will discuss this topic—a contract that you will fulfill. When you read over your draft, check to see that you have kept all parts of your promise.

It's best to start with a working thesis that may change or become clearer as you write. Having a working thesis as you start will help you focus your thinking and research, keep you on track as you find and develop the content of your essay, and assist in determining the audience, purpose, and type of support you will need. Later, you can revise the thesis.

There are two parts to an effective thesis statement, a topic that states the subject and a comment that makes an important point about the topic:

<u>Genetically modified foods</u>   <u>have not been shown to</u>
    (topic)   (comment)
<u>cause health problems in people who eat them.</u>

An effective thesis statement should have a topic of potential interest to your readers, be as specific as possible, and be limited enough to make it manageable. For example, for a short paper on citizens' right to privacy (maybe limited to several pages), you can't include discussions of the many ways privacy can be invaded (phone taps, e-mail, videotaping in the workplace, etc.). Similarly, for a paper of maybe fifteen to twenty pages, you aren't likely to find enough material to write about if you want to argue that Harry Potter books appeal to children's imaginations.

Consider this thesis statement. Is it well formulated?

The beetle is a very interesting insect.

The topic of beetles isn't likely to interest a broad range of readers, the comment isn't specific because we don't know what the writer means by "interesting," and we don't know what kind of support the writer will offer. Thus, this is not an effective thesis statement.

Organization

As you read over your draft, note the central idea of each paragraph (the topic sentence) and ask yourself if each paragraph contributes to the larger thesis in some way and if each paragraph leads logically to the next one. You want to avoid gaps or jumps in the development of your thesis that might confuse the reader. One way to check this is to look at the topic sentences of your paper as an outline. Do those sentences, once collected, make a smooth, coherent outline?

Development

Be sure you have enough details, examples, specifics, supporting evidence, and information to support your thesis. You may need to delete material that is not relevant or add material that will strengthen your thesis and help you achieve your purpose. Try to read the paper as an uninformed reader would and ask yourself what else you'd need to know.

Paragraph length

Paragraphs are the large building blocks of the paper. As you look over your draft, check to see that the paragraphs are of the same approximate length on the page. If you have a paragraph that takes most of a page, followed by a paragraph that has only two sentences, you probably need to make the paragraphs more equal in length. Check to see that a long paragraph doesn't cover too much content or that a short paragraph needs more specifics.

Transitions between sentences and paragraphs

Transitions connect or knit sentences and paragraphs together into a smooth whole. Like road signals, they indicate where the writing is heading and keep your reader following along easily. Check to see that you've supplied the needed connectors to indicate how your writing is moving forward. (See section 9 for a list of transitions you can use.)

Introductions and conclusions

The introduction brings the reader into your world, builds interest in your subject, and announces the thesis or topic of the paper. Sometimes, writers write the introduction after revising the rest of the paper and clarifying their topic through their writing and revising.

The conclusion of the paper signals the end is approaching and helps the reader to put the whole paper in perspective. You can look backward and offer a conclusion that summarizes the content or refers to something in the introduction. Or you can look forward and offer advice, suggestions, or actions the reader can take, based on what you have presented.

Arguments

Reading and writing persuasive arguments are very likely to be part of your everyday life. You send out applications and resumes, make written requests, and want to persuade others to accept your ideas. You also read advertisements, hear political speeches, and read requests for support and donations. To compose effective arguments, consider the following:

hint

Composing Persuasive Arguments

- **Show that your motives are reasonable and worthwhile.** Explain to your audience that you are arguing for something that is worthwhile and that shares the audience's motives.

- **Gain your audience's trust.** Show that you are credible and can be trusted to be truthful and that you are knowledgeable about your subject.

- **Avoid vague or exaggerated claims.** Vague arguments such as "everyone says" or exaggerated claims such as "no one listens to television news programs" raise doubts about the writer or speaker as a credible person.

- **Find common ground with your audience.** When you find goals and interests that you and your audience share, your audience is more likely to listen to your arguments.

- **Use various types of appeals.** Logical appeals are grounded in reason, data, and evidence; emotional appeals seek to arouse sympathy, patriotism, pride, or other feelings based on values, beliefs, and motives; ethical proof appeals to the audience's impressions, opinions, and judgments about the person making the argument.

- **Be sure your topic is arguable.** Topics for persuasion are always those that can be argued, that have two or more sides. No one can argue that many people have lost jobs that have been outsourced overseas. This is a fact that can be checked. But it may be argued that government can or should stem the tide of these jobs being lost to other countries.

Writing about literature

When we write about various types of literature (stories, poems, plays, novels), we understand them more deeply and learn more about the world as seen through the eyes of the writer.

hint

Analyzing Literature

We should react to literature through a variety of ways that involve analysis:

- Analyze the theme in a work or the plot and how it displays the theme.

- Analyze characters. Consider their behavior, how they are described, what they say, how they interact with each other, and how this all fits into the plot or theme of the work or its setting.

- Analyze the structure of the work. Is it chronological? Does it skip around? Does the writer provide clues as to what will happen?

- Analyze the narrator. Who is telling the story, someone outside the events or one of the characters? Does the narrator tell the reader the characters' thoughts? What is the narrator's attitude or tone?

- Look at the genre of the work. Is it tragedy, comedy, sonnet form, mystery, science fiction? How does this work compare to others of its type? Does it blend several types of literature? Is it an effective example of this type of work?

- Analyze the work in terms of the historical or cultural background. How does the work reflect values and beliefs of the time in which it is set or was written? Would contemporary readers interpret it differently than readers at the time it was written?

- Analyze the work in terms of gender. How does the work portray women or men? Does it define their roles in traditional or contemporary ways?

- Focus on the reactions of the audience. Why do readers respond as they do? If the meaning of the text is constructed by readers, what is a reader response to this work?

(continued)

> • Resist the obvious meaning of the work. Read skeptically, look for internal inconsistencies, focus on ambiguities of the work. How would you interpret the work?

hint

Pitfalls in Writing about Literature

- Some writers make the mistake of writing a plot summary instead of an analysis. Summarize only when you need to, to support a point.

- Be sure to include information that the reader needs. Don't assume information can be left out because the reader (especially the instructor) has read the work. Part of the purpose of the paper is to show that you have read and understand the work and that you have learned what has been taught in the course.

1b   LOCs (Later Order Concerns)

hint

LOCs (Proofreading Checklist)

After your draft is well on the way to being completed, check for Later Order Concerns (LOCs) that should be considered as you edit and proofread.

When you have finished your major revisions and checked the HOCs (section 1a), look more closely at words, sentences, and punctuation for problem areas that detract from your credibility as a writer. As you make your own list of problems to check for, consider whether you need to check for these common problems:

fragments	(see section 11, page 34)
subject-verb agreement	(see section 13a, page 37)
verb endings	(see section 13b, page 42)
verb tenses	(see section 13b, page 46)
comma splices and run-on sentences	(see section 12, page 36)

misplaced or omitted apostrophes	(see section 21, page 76)
pronoun reference	(see section 14c, page 53)
omitted words	(see section 34, page 117)
omitted commas	(see section 19, page 69)
unnecessary commas	(see section 19, page 69)
spelling errors	(see section 28, page 99)

1c   Strategies for checking on HOCs and LOCs

Find writing strategies that are effective for you, such as the following:

- Have someone (such as a tutor in your writing center who will help with this) read your paper aloud as you listen and look at it, or read the paper aloud yourself. You'll see problems that won't be as evident when you read silently.

- Put the draft away for a while so that when you read, the paper is not as fresh in your mind. To revise effectively, you need to have some distance from the paper so that you can more easily identify readers' concerns.

- Try to put yourself in the place of your intended readers and think about what they would want to know, what they might object to in your arguments, what counterarguments they would make, what questions they would have. Ask yourself if your paper responds adequately to these considerations.

- For proofreading you need to help your eyes slow down and see each word. (Readers tend to see whole groups of words at once.) Try sliding a card down the page as you read because that permits your eyes and ears to work together.

- Proofread for spelling by reading backward, either from the end of the paper to the beginning or from the right side of the line to the left. Then you are not focusing on the meaning of the sentences and can notice smaller matters such as word choice, punctuation, and spelling. Computer spell checkers will catch some, but not all, spelling errors.

- Don't depend on computerized grammar checkers. They may help slightly, but they cannot analyze language well enough to check completely for grammar problems, and the options suggested are sometimes not appropriate.

- Draw up a personal list of problem areas and keep those in mind as you reread your draft.

1d   Strategies for using computers

Word processing on a computer can help as you write and as you check your paper. Try the following strategies to see which are helpful for you:

- Copy the topic sentences from each paragraph and put them in an outline onscreen. If you have any questions about the organization, cut and paste and see if there are other arrangements you think are more effective.

- Be sure to use a spell checker because it is especially useful in catching typos. But remember that spell checkers can't find all spelling problems. They cannot, for example, distinguish between "it's" and "its" or "here" and "hear" to see if you have used the right form of these sound-alike words.

- As you write, highlight in some way (such as boldface) problem areas or phrases you have questions about. Then you can find them later and consider them then.

- If you think it might be better to delete a chunk of text, cut and paste it to a new file or the end of the paper while you see if the paper is better without it. By putting it in a separate file, you can save it for later use or retrieve it if you decide you need it.

- If a fresh idea pops into your mind as you're writing but probably belongs elsewhere in the paper, write that in a separate file. (Some word processing programs will permit you to make notes to yourself as you write that are not visible in the main text.)

- Many writers need to print out a hard copy of the paper as it develops to get a better sense of the whole paper.

- To check on paragraph length, switch to page or print view so that you can see a whole page on the monitor. See if the paragraphs look about the same length.

- Working with a copy of your file, hit the return key after each period so that each sentence looks like a separate paragraph. If all the sentences are approximately the same length, you may need to consider varying your sentences more (see section 4). If most of the sentences begin the same way (with the subject of the main clause), you need to think about using different sentence patterns.

1e   Oral and multimedia presentations

Planning: Begin your planning as you would for writing a paper. Think about your goal, your purpose, and your audience. In addition, think about whether you want to read from a prepared talk or an outline or work from memory. If you have been given a time limit for your talk, write a paragraph or so and then read it aloud slowly and clearly to get some idea of how long it takes to cover that much material. That will give you a fairly accurate estimate of how much material to prepare. If time permits, practice in front of a mirror and time yourself. Consider whether you want to allow time for people to ask questions, too. If you read from a prepared talk, type it in large print and double-space so that your eye can follow along easily. Or you can work from note cards or an outline. If you use an outline, consider preparing a visual with the outline that can be shown in some way such as with an overhead projector or PowerPoint software (or distributed as a handout) so that the audience can follow along. Visuals can make the talk more interesting, so try to incorporate some. Be sure the visual is large enough for everyone in the audience to read easily. (For more on preparing visuals, see section 39.) Whether or not you include visuals, consider preparing handouts, too, as audiences often appreciate reminders of your talk and additional information they can take away with them after the talk.

Delivering: Begin with a strong opening, perhaps using humor, a memorable quotation, a question, or an interesting anecdote. Use your body effectively by maintaining eye contact as much as possible. Don't stand behind a lectern or podium. Instead, move from one side of the room to the other so that everyone can see you, no matter where they are sitting, and use natural gestures as you speak. Audiences are more likely to pay attention when you don't read your talk, so if you prefer to read, try to look up occasionally or add remarks not in the text of the talk.

To help your audience see the organization of your talk, include an overview of what you will be speaking about and how it will be organized. This is easily done if you use handouts or visuals, but if that's not convenient, as you talk indicate where and how each part of the presentation fits into the whole. Be sure to emphasize your main point. If you present data, lists, or other information that the audience needs to follow along (or to remember after your talk), include that in the handouts. Don't be afraid to repeat your main ideas. When people listen instead of reading your writing, they are less likely to retain all of your points.

If you are going to give a presentation with multimedia, there are several things you need to do before you give your talk:

- Rehearse the presentation with the multimedia included so that you get used to incorporating it as you speak.

- Before your presentation, test out all your equipment and be sure you know how to operate it and whether it works. Learn how to work any controls or ask someone to handle that for you.

- Have a backup plan for what you will do if there are problems with the technology. Even if all the equipment worked during rehearsal, you may find problems occur while you're talking.

Calming down: Speaking in front of groups is bound to make anyone nervous. But use that nervousness to your advantage and think of it as extra energy that is going to help you. Some people overcome stage fright by picturing the people in the audience completing some everyday act, like brushing their teeth or putting on socks. That helps to humanize those faces staring at you and can calm you down. Others practice relaxation exercises or do some deep breathing.

Two useful Web sites for public speaking include:

- University of Hawai'i Maui Community College, "Speakers' Page," <http://www.hawaii.edu/mauispeech/>

- Humboldt State University, "Internet Resources for Speech Preparation," <http://sorrel.humboldt.edu/~speech/speeches.html>

II
Sentence Choices

Contents of this section

QUESTION AND CORRECT

	SECTION	PAGE
✦ Why shouldn't I use negatives such as "no" and "not" in my writing?	2a	16
✦ Why is "don't want no paper" wrong?	2b	16
✦ What are some other negatives I should watch out for?	2	16
✦ What's the best order for putting information in a sentence? Why?	2c	17

2

Clarity

2a Positive instead of negative

Put information in the positive because negative statements are harder to understand than positive ones.

Unclear negative: Less attention is paid to commercials that lack human interest stories.

Revised: People pay more attention to commercials with human interest stories.

Negatives can also make the writer seem more evasive or unsure.

Evasive negative: Governor Petros is not often heard to favor raising the minimum wage.

Revised: Governor Petros prefers keeping the minimum wage at its present level.

2b Double negatives

Use only one negative at a time in your sentences. Double negatives are grammatically incorrect and may be difficult to understand.

Double negative: They don't want no phone calls.

Revised: They don't want any phone calls.

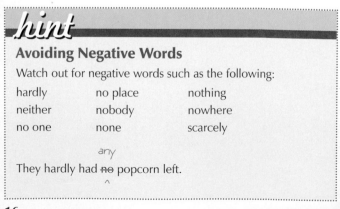

hint

Avoiding Negative Words

Watch out for negative words such as the following:

hardly	no place	nothing
neither	nobody	nowhere
no one	none	scarcely

any

They hardly had ~~no~~ popcorn left.

2c   Known information to new or unknown information

Start your sentences with information that is known or generally familiar to your reader before you introduce new or unknown material.

Familiar ———► Unfamiliar

Familiar to new: When I visit my grandmother, she often has an old book from her childhood days to show me.

(This sentence should be easy to understand.)

New to familiar: An old book from her childhood days is something my grandmother often shows me when I visit.

(This sentence takes longer to understand and is less clear.)

2d   Verbs instead of nouns

Actions expressed as verbs are more easily understood and usually more concise than actions named as nouns.

Unnecessary noun forms: Pay raises are a motivation improvement.

Revised: Pay raises improve motivation.

Using Verbs Instead of Nouns

Try rereading your sentences to see which nouns could be changed to verbs.

Some noun forms	Verbs to use instead
The determination of	They determine
The approval of	They approve
The preparation of	They prepare
The utilization of	They use
The analysis of	They analyze

2e   Intended subject as sentence subject

The real subject (or doer of the action in the verb) should be the grammatical subject of the sentence. Sometimes the real subject can get buried in prepositional phrases or other less noticeable places.

Buried subject: It was the preference of the instructor to begin each lecture with a quiz.

(The grammatical subject here is "it." Who begins each lecture? The instructor.)

Revised: The instructor preferred to begin each lecture with a quiz.

3

Conciseness

To be concise, eliminate the following:

- what your readers do not need to know
- what your readers already know
- whatever doesn't further the purpose of your paper

Sometimes writers are wordy when they are tempted to include everything they know about a subject, add a description of how they found their information (to impress readers with how hard they've worked to get the information), or add words they think will make their writing sound more formal or academic.

Strategies to eliminate unnecessary words include:

- **Avoid repetition.**   Some phrases, such as the following, say the same thing twice:

  first beginning   9 a.m. in the morning
  circular in shape   true facts

return again   really and truly
green in color   each and every

- **Avoid fillers.**   Some phrases, such as the following, add little or nothing to your meaning:

  in view of the fact that   due to the fact that
  I am going to discuss   there are (or) is
  the topic that I will explain here   it is my feeling that

  ~~I am going to discuss~~ ^T^ the cloning of human beings~~, which~~

  is a subject with many difficult ethical questions.

- **Combine sentences.**   When the same nouns appear in two sentences, combine the sentences.

  Global warming is a critically important topic. ~~Global~~ ^and^

  ~~warming~~ has been the subject of recent TV specials, government regulations, and conferences.

- **Eliminate *who, which*, and *that*.**
  The marking pen ~~that was~~ on my desk is gone.

- **Turn phrases and clauses into adjectives and adverbs.**
  The football player who was graceful = the graceful football player
  The building built out of cement = the cement building
  The entrance to the station = the station entrance

- **Remove excess nouns and change to verbs whenever possible.**

  He ~~made the statement that he was in agreement with~~ ^agreed^

  ~~the concept~~ that inflation could be controlled.

- **Use active rather than passive.**   (See section 7, page 23.)

  The ~~figures were~~ checked ~~by the research department.~~
  ^research department^ ^the figures.^

4

Variety

A series of short sentences or sentences with the same sub-ject-verb word order can be monotonous and sound choppy. Try these strategies for adding variety.

- **Combine short, choppy sentences.** Connect two sentences into one longer sentence with one subject and two verbs, or a comma and coordinating conjunction (see section 12, page 36), or a semicolon (see section 18, page 67).

The school band performed at the local Apple

Festival. ~~They~~ *, and they* were a great success.

Tuck a phrase, clause, or sentence inside a related sentence.

The school band *, who* performed at the local Apple

Festival. ~~They~~ *,* were a great success.

- **Rearrange sentence order.** Often, a series of sentences that sound choppy all have a subject-verb-object order. You can make one sentence depend on another or add or change phrases and clauses to break up the monotonous sound.

Choppy: The reporter asked each candidate the same question. He wanted to compare their campaign promises. They all evaded his questions. He wrote a story about their lack of answers.

Revised: Because the reporter wanted to compare the candidates' campaign promises, he asked each one the same question. Hearing them evade his questions, he wrote a story about their lack of answers.

5

Voice (Formal and Informal)

In writing, an appropriate voice is one that fits the level of formality of your paper and your subject. Just as you don't wear a suit or dress when you go on a picnic or a sweatshirt to a formal dinner, you should match your word choices to the type of paper you are writing.

Formal documents such as research papers, reports, and applications avoid slang but may include some technical language, or jargon, appropriate to the field and the intended readers. Such documents are normally written in the third person, using "he" and "they."

Informal documents such as e-mail and letters to friends, informal essays, and some memos may include more informal word choices (for example, "kids" instead of "children") and frequent contractions, and they are normally written in the first person, using "I."

Compare these recommendations:

Informal: Be sure to see that new Brad Pitt movie. I saw it last week, and it's great!

Formal: The laminate is the recommended choice for this product because test results show that it holds up well under stress and heat.

Slang

Slang words may be shared by a small group or may be generally known. Some slang enters the general vocabulary, such as "cab" or "yuppie," and some eventually disappears or becomes outdated, such as "far out" or "BMOC" (Big Man on Campus). It is usually too informal for most written work.

Jargon

Jargon words are specialized terms used by those in the same profession or reasonably familiar with the field to refer quickly to complex concepts. For someone who is knowledgeable about computers, "beta test" and "bitmaps" are useful technical terms when writing to someone else likely to know those terms. Such shorthand vocabulary should be used only when you are sure your readers will be familiar with the words.

The term "jargon" is also applied to pompous language that is inflated and unnecessarily formal. The result is wordy prose that is hard to read and makes the writer sound pretentious.

Pompous: She was inordinately predisposed to render her perspective on all matters of national and international import.

Revised: She frequently offered her opinion on world affairs.

6

Mixed Constructions

Mixed constructions are caused by mismatches when fitting parts of a sentence together. A writer can start off in one direction and then switch to another, causing grammar or logic problems in the sentence.

Mixed: For groups who want to reduce violence on television, students carrying knives to school are acting out what they see on the television screen.

Revised: Groups who want to reduce violence on television claim that students carrying knives to school are acting out what they see on the television screen.

Dangling modifiers

Some mixed constructions are caused by dangling modifiers— phrases or clauses that should modify the subject but don't.

Dangling: After <u>finishing</u> her degree, the <u>search</u> for a job began.

(This sentence says that the <u>search,</u> the subject of the sentence, <u>finished</u> her degree.)

Revised: After <u>finishing</u> her degree, <u>she</u> began the search for a job.

Mismatched subjects and predicates

Sometimes the subject and predicate don't match or fit together.

Mismatched: <u>Driver education</u> in high schools <u>assumes</u> that parents can pay the costs involved.

(<u>Driver education,</u> the subject, can't make assumptions about anything.)

Revised: High school administrators assume that parents can pay the costs involved for driver education programs.

7

Active and Passive Verbs

An active verb expresses the action completed by the subject. A passive verb expresses action done to the subject.

The active voice is usually more direct, clearer, and more concise than passive. However, sometimes the passive is a better choice.

Active: <u>Paul</u> **drove** the <u>car</u>.

(The verb is <u>drove,</u> and <u>Paul,</u> the subject, did the driving.)

Passive: The <u>car</u> <u>was driven</u> by Paul.

(The verb is <u>was driven,</u> and <u>the car,</u> the subject, was acted upon.)

Active verbs are clearer than passive because they indicate who is doing the action and add a strong sense of immediateness and vigor. In a sentence with a passive verb, the "by the" phrase where the doer of the action is indicated may be left out or put far from the verb. Compare these sentences:

Passive: The photographs showing the tornado were snapped in a hurry by me.

Active: I hurriedly snapped the photographs of the tornado.

Because active verbs add directness and force, they are often a better choice for sentences containing action that begin with "there is" or "there are."

Original:	Revised:
There were six victims of the crime whose accounts of what happened agreed.	Six of the crime victims gave the same accounts of the crime.

However, there are occasions to use the passive:

- When the doer of the action is not known or not important:

  The water temperature was recorded.

- When you want to focus on the receiver of the action:

  Historical fiction is not widely read.

- When you want to focus on the action, not the doer:

  The records have been destroyed.

- When you want to avoid blaming or giving credit:

  The candidate concedes that the election is lost.

- When you want a tone of objectivity or wish to exclude yourself:

  The complete report was drafted and on the president's desk yesterday.

8

Parallelism

Parallel structure exists when the same grammatical form or structure is used for equal ideas in a list or in a comparison. That similar form helps your reader locate the similar

or compared ideas. Often, the equal elements repeat words
or sounds.

Parallel: The computer manual explained <u>how to boot up</u>

(1)

<u>the hard drive</u> and <u>how to install the software.</u>

(2)

*Phrases (1) and (2) are parallel because both start with
<u>how to.</u>*

Parallel: <u>Watching Walt fumble with his headgear</u> was as

(1)

funny as <u>seeing him try to skate</u>.

(2)

*Phrases (1) and (2) are parallel because both start with
<u>–ing</u> verb forms.*

Parallel: Three keys to marketing success include the
            following:

<u>To listen</u> to the customer's wishes

(1)

<u>To offer</u> several alternatives

(2)

<u>To motivate</u> the customer to buy

(3)

*Phrases (1), (2), and (3) are parallel items in a list because
all begin with <u>to</u> + verb.*

Parallel structure is also needed when you link items
using the following:

both . . . as	*either . . . or*
not only . . . but	*neither . . . nor*

coordinating conjunctions: *and, but, for, or, nor, so, yet*
comparisons using *than* or *as*

Parallel: Job opportunities are not only <u>increasing</u> in the

(1)

health fields but <u>expanding</u> in many areas of manufacturing

(2)

as well.

*Phrases (1) and (2) are parallel items using <u>–ing</u> verbs
linked with <u>but</u>.*

Faulty parallelism is not only grammatically incorrect but can also lead to possible lack of clarity.

Dr. Hemenez explained that either <u>starting</u> the
(1)

avoiding
treatment or <u>to avoid</u> surgery was impossible.
(2) ^

Tara wondered whether it was better <u>to tell</u> her mother
(1)

to fix
that she had wrecked the car or maybe <u>fixing</u> it herself.
^ (2)

---

hint

Parallel Structure

As you proofread, do the following:

- Listen to the sound when you are linking equal ideas or comparing two or more elements. (Parallelism can add emphasis to your writing and public speaking by that repetition of sound.)
- Visualize similar elements in a list and check to see if they are in the same grammatical structure.

9

Transitions

Transitions are words and phrases that build bridges to connect sentences, parts of sentences, and paragraphs together. These bridges show relationships and add smoothness (or "flow") to your writing.

There are several types of transitions you can use:

- Repetition of a key term or phrase

    Delegates at the conference could not agree on the degree of danger from <u>global warming</u>. But no one disputed the existence of <u>global warming</u>.

- Synonyms

    The <u>movie industry</u> expanded to produce a variety of forms of entertainment, such as television films and music videos. But <u>Hollywood</u> will always have movies as its main focus.

- Pronouns

    <u>College tuition</u> has been increasing rapidly for several years. But <u>it</u> still does not finance needed improvements on many campuses.

- Transition words and phrases

    The investigators looking into the cause of the pollution pinpointed one farm. <u>Therefore</u>, the owner was forced to reduce his use of the fertilizers that were washing into the stream. <u>In the meantime</u>, the local chemical plant continued its dumping practices.

TRANSITIONS

Adding:	and, besides, in addition, also, too, furthermore, third
Comparing:	similarly, likewise, in the same way, at the same time
Contrasting:	but, yet, on the other hand, instead, whereas, although
Emphasizing:	indeed, in fact, above all, and also, obviously, clearly
Ending:	after all, finally, in sum
Giving examples:	for example, for instance, namely, specifically, that is
Showing cause and effect:	thus, therefore, consequently, as a result, accordingly, so

TRANSITIONS (*continued*)

Showing place or direction:	over, above, next to, beneath, to the left, in the distance
Showing time:	meanwhile, later, afterward, now, finally, in the meantime
Summarizing:	in brief, on the whole, in conclusion, in other words

hint

Words That Start Sentences

Although some instructors prefer that you don't use or overuse the transitions "But" or "And" as sentence starters, it is not wrong to use them. Any word can start a sentence.

10

Nonsexist Language

Language that favors the male noun or pronoun or excludes females is sexist. To avoid such language, do the following:

- Use alternatives to <u>man</u>:

man	**alternative**
man	person
mankind	people, human beings
man-made	machine-made, synthetic
to man	to operate

- Use alternatives for job titles:

man	**alternative**
chairman	chair, chairperson
Dear Sir:	Dear Editor, Dear Sales Representative
mailman	letter carrier, postal worker

policeman	police officer
fireman	firefighter
steward, stewardess	flight attendant
congressman	congressional representative, member of Congress

- Use the plural instead.

Sexist: Give the customer <u>his</u> receipt immediately.

Revised: Give customers <u>their</u> receipts immediately.

- Reword and eliminate the male pronoun.

Sexist: Give the customer <u>his</u> receipt.

Revised: Give the customer <u>the</u> receipt.

- Replace the male pronoun with <u>one</u>, <u>you</u>, <u>he</u> or <u>she</u>, and so on.

Sexist: The student can select <u>his</u> preferred residence hall.

Revised: The student can select <u>his</u> or <u>her</u> preferred residence hall.

- Address the reader directly.

Sexist: The applicant should mail two copies of <u>his</u> form by Monday.

Revised: Mail two copies of <u>your</u> form by Monday.

---

hint

Using "Everyone . . . His"

For indefinite pronouns such as "everyone" and "anybody," the traditional practice is to use the masculine singular to refer back to that pronoun:

Traditional: Everyone brought his own pen and paper.

To avoid the male pronoun, which is seen by many people as sexist, you can use the strategies listed in section 10. Others, however, such as the National Council of Teachers of English, accept the plural as a way to avoid sexist language:

Everyone brought their own pen and paper.

III
Sentence Grammar

Contents of this section

QUESTION AND CORRECT

11

Fragments

A sentence fragment is an incomplete sentence. To recognize a fragment consider the basic requirements of a sentence:

- A sentence is a group of words with at least one independent clause.

- An independent clause has a subject and complete verb plus an object or a complement if needed.

- An independent clause can stand alone as a thought, even though it may need other sentences before and after it to clarify the thoughts being expressed.

Independent clause: Jaime's picture was in the newspaper.

Independent clause: He scored six three-point baskets during the game.

(We don't know who "he" is in this sentence, but a pronoun can be a subject, and we don't know which game is being referred to. But those bits of information, if needed, would be explained in accompanying sentences. The clause has a subject ["he"], a verb ["scored"], and an object ["baskets"].)

Not an independent clause: Because he scored six three-point baskets during the game.

(Say that clause out loud, and you will hear that it's not a complete sentence. The problem is that we don't know the result of the "because" clause.)

Not an independent clause: Luis who was one of my closest friends in third and fourth grade and is now moving with his family to another city.

(This is not a complete sentence because it has a subject, "Luis," but no main verb that tells us what Luis did. The verbs "was" and "is moving" belong to another subject [the pronoun "who"] and tell us what "who" did.)

Some fragments are unintended:

Unintended fragment: There were some complications with her phone bill. <u>Such as two calls she did not make and a long-distance charge for a local call.</u>

(The second sentence is an unintended fragment because it has no subject and verb. It is a phrase that got disconnected from the independent clause that came before it.)

Unintended fragment: The doctor's recommendation that I get more sleep because I was becoming very stressed out while taking too many classes which I need for my major.

(The subject is "recommendation" but there is no main verb to complete that thought.)

Some fragments are intentional when they are used to add an effect such as emphasis or sudden change in tempo. However, intended fragments should be used only when the writing clearly indicates that the writer chose to include a fragment.

Intended fragment: Never had there been such a decisive victory in the school's history of participating in the tournament, and no one stayed at home that night when the team's bus pulled into town. <u>No one.</u>

(The fragment "No one" is used here to add emphasis.)

hint

Avoiding Fragments

HINT 1

To proofread for fragments caused by misplaced periods, read your paper backward, from the last sentence to the first. You will notice a fragment more easily when you hear it without the sentence to which it belongs. Most, but not all, fragments occur after the main clause.

HINT 2

Some fragments are caused by a marker word typically found at the beginning of the clause that requires a second clause to finish the thought. Consider a marker word such as "if" and how it affects the clause:

If A happens ⟶ ?

(continued)

When you hear that, you want to know what B is, that is, what the result is if A happens. Watch for other, similar marker words such as the following:

after	although	because	before	during
if	since	unless	when	while

12

Comma Splices and Fused Sentences

A comma splice and a fused sentence (also called a run-on sentence) are punctuation problems in compound sentences. (A compound sentence is one that joins two or more independent clauses—clauses that could have been sentences by themselves.)

To avoid comma splices and fused sentences, note the three patterns for commas and semicolons in compound sentences:

1. Join an independent clause with a comma and one of the seven joining words listed here:

   (Independent clause)(,) *and* (independent clause).

   > *but*
   > *for*
   > *or*
   > *nor*
   > *so*
   > *yet*

   No one was home, but the door was open.

2. Join two independent clauses with a semicolon and no joining words:

   (Independent clause)(;) (independent clause).

   No one was home; the door was open.

3. Join two independent clauses with a semicolon and any connecting word other than one of the seven joining words for commas listed above: "and," "but," "for," "or," "nor," "so," or "yet."

(Independent clause)(;) *however*, (independent clause).

> *therefore,*
> *consequently,*
> *thus,*

No one was home; however, the door was open.

If you don't use one of these three patterns for compound sentences, the sentence will have a comma splice:

Comma splice: No one was home, the door was open.

---

hint
Using Commas in Compound Sentences

HINT 1

When punctuating compound sentences, think of the comma as only half of the needed connection to tie two independent clauses together. The other half is the connecting word. You need both the comma and the connecting word.

HINT 2

Don't put commas before every "and" or "but" in your sentences. "And" and "but" have other uses in sentences in addition to joining two independent clauses.

13

Subjects and Verbs

13a   **Subject-verb agreement**

Subjects and verbs should agree in number and person.

- To agree in number, the verb used with a plural subject should have a plural ending, and a verb used with a singular subject should have a singular ending.

The customer   orders

(singular subject)   (singular verb)

The customers   order

(plural subject)   (plural verb)

- To agree in person, the verb should be in the same person (first person = "I/we"; second person = "you"; third person = "he/they") as the subject.

I know   you know   she knows   they know

(For verb tense endings, see page 46.)

- Some subjects are hard to find because they are buried among many other words. In that case, disregard the prepositional phrases, modifiers, and other surrounding words.

Almost every <u>one</u> of the applicants for the job who came
                (subject)

for interviews <u>is</u> highly qualified.
                (verb)

---

hint

Subject-Verb Agreement

HINT 1

The letter *s* is used both for subject endings (plural) and for verb endings (singular). Because a plural subject can't have a singular verb, and a singular verb can't have a plural subject, the letter *s* should not normally be the ending for both the subject and the verb.

chime⃥s ring   the chime ring⃥s

(continued)

> **HINT 2**
>
> When you check subject-verb endings, start by finding the verb. The main verb is the word that changes when you change the time of the sentence, from past to present or present to past. Then, ask yourself "who" or "what" is doing that action, and you will find the subject.
>
> **HINT 3**
>
> To find a subject buried among other words and phrases, start by eliminating phrases starting with prepositions; "who," "that," or "which" clauses; or words such as the following:
>
> | | | |
> |---|---|---|
> | including | along with | together with |
> | accompanied by | in addition to | as well as |
> | except | with | no less than |

Compound subjects

Subjects joined by "and" take a plural verb (X and Y = more than one).

The (stereo) and the (speaker) are sold as a unit.

Sometimes, words joined by "and" act together as a unit and are thought of as one thing. If so, use a singular verb.

(Peanut butter and jelly) is his favorite sandwich spread.

"Either/or" subjects

When the subject words are joined by "either . . . or," "neither . . . nor," or "not only . . . but also," the verb agrees with the closest subject word.

Either (Maylene) or her (children) are going to bed early.

Indefinites as subjects

Indefinite words with singular meanings such as "each," "every," and "any" take a singular subject when (1) they are the subject word or (2) they precede the subject word.

Each (book) on the shelves is marked with a barcode.

However, when indefinite words such as "none," "some," "most," or "all" are the subject, the number of the verb depends on the meaning of the subject.

Some of the movie is difficult to understand.

Some of those movies are difficult to understand.

Collective nouns and amounts as subjects

Nouns that refer to groups or a collection (such as "family," "committee," or "group") are collective nouns. When the collective noun refers to the group acting as a whole or single unit, the verb is singular.

Our family needs a new car.

Occasionally, a collective noun refers to a member of a group acting individually, not as a unit. In that case, the verb is plural.

The committee are happy with each other's decisions.

Plural words as subjects

Some words that have an –s ending, such as "news" or "mathematics," are thought of as a single unit and take a singular verb.

Physics is. . . .   Economics is. . . .   Measles is. . . .

Some words, such as those in the following examples, are treated as plural and take a plural verb, even though they refer to one thing. (In many cases, though, there are two parts to these things.)

Jeans are. . . .   Pants are. . . .   Scissors are. . . .

Titles, company names, and terms as subjects

For titles of written works, names of companies, and words used as terms, use singular verbs.

All the King's Men is the book assigned for this week.

General Foods is hiring people for its new plant.

"Cheers" is a word he often uses when leaving.

Linking verbs

Linking verbs agree with the subject rather than the word that follows (the complement).

Those poems are my favorites.

The poem is their favorite.

"There is/there are/it"

When a sentence begins with "there is," "there are," or "it," the verb depends on the complement (the word that follows it).

There is a surprise ending to that story.

There are surprise endings in many of her stories.

"Who, which, that," and "one of . . . who/which/that" as subjects

When "who," "which," and "that" are used as subjects, the verb agrees with the previous word it refers to (the antecedent).

They are the students who <u>want</u> to change the parking rules.

He is the student who <u>wants</u> to change the parking rules.

In the phrase "one of those who," it is necessary to decide whether the "who," "which," or "that" refers only to the one or to the whole group. Only then can you decide whether the verb is singular or plural.

Mr. Liu is one of the salespersons who <u>know</u> the product.

(In this case, Mr. Liu is part of a large group, those salespersons who know the product.)

Mr. Liu is the only one of the salespersons who <u>knows</u> the product.

13b   Verbs

Regular and irregular verb forms

Verbs that add *–ed* for the past tense and the past participle are regular verbs.

I <u>talk</u>   I <u>talked</u>   I have <u>talked</u>
(present)   *(past)*   *(past participle)*

The past participle is the form that has a helping verb such as "has" or "had."

Verb Forms (Regular)

	Present	Past	Future
Simple	I walk	I walked	I will walk
Progressive	I am walking	I was walking	I will be walking
Perfect	I have walked	I had walked	I will have walked
Perfect Progressive	I have been walking	I had been walking	I will have been walking

Verb Forms (Irregular)

	Present		Past	
Verb	singular	plural	singular	plural
to be	I am you are he, she, it is	we are you are they are	I was you were he, she, it was	we were you were they were
to have	I have you have he, she, it has	we have you have they have	I had you had he, she, it had	we had you had they had
to do	I do you do he, she, it does	we do you do they do	I did you did he, she, it did	we did you did they did

Some of the frequently used irregular verb forms include the following:

Irregular Verbs

Base (Present)	Past	Past Participle
awake	awoke	awoken
be	was, were	been
beat	beat	beaten
become	became	become
begin	began	begun
bet	bet	bet
bite	bit	bitten (or) bit
bleed	bled	bled
blow	blew	blown
break	broke	broken
bring	brought	brought
build	built	built
burst	burst	burst
buy	bought	bought
catch	caught	caught
choose	chose	chosen
come	came	come
cost	cost	cost
cut	cut	cut
dig	dug	dug
do	did	done
draw	drew	drawn
drink	drank	drunk
drive	drove	driven
eat	ate	eaten
fall	fell	fallen
feed	fed	fed
feel	felt	felt

(continued)

Base (Present)	Past	Past Participle
fight	fought	fought
find	found	found
fling	flung	flung
fly	flew	flown
forbid	forbade	forbidden
forget	forgot	forgotten
freeze	froze	frozen
get	got	gotten
give	gave	given
go	went	gone
grow	grew	grown
hang	hung	hung
have	had	had
hear	heard	heard
hit	hit	hit
hold	held	held
hurt	hurt	hurt
keep	kept	kept
know	knew	known
lay	laid	laid
lie	lay	lain
make	made	made
mean	meant	meant
meet	met	met
mistake	mistook	mistaken
pay	paid	paid
prove	proved	proved (or) proven
put	put	put
read	read	read
ride	rode	ridden
ring	rang	rung
rise	rose	risen
run	ran	run
say	said	said
see	saw	seen
sell	sold	sold

(continued)

Base (Present)	Past	Past Participle
send	sent	sent
set	set	set
shake	shook	shaken
shine	shone	shone
shoot	shot	shot
shrink	shrank	shrunk
shut	shut	shut
sing	sang	sung
sit	sat	sit
sleep	slept	slept
slide	slid	slid
speak	spoke	spoken
spend	spent	spent
spin	spun	spun
split	split	split
spread	spread	spread
spring	sprang	sprung
stand	stood	stood
steal	stole	stolen
stick	stuck	stuck
stink	stank	stunk
strike	struck	struck
swear	swore	sworn
sweep	swept	swept
swim	swam	swum
swing	swung	swung
take	took	taken
teach	taught	taught
tear	tore	torn
tell	told	told
understand	understood	understood
wear	wore	worn
weep	wept	wept
win	won	won
wind	wound	wound
write	wrote	written

"Lie/lay," "sit/set," "rise/raise"

Three sets of verbs that cause problems are "lie/lay," "sit/set," and "rise/raise." Because they are related in meaning and sound, they are sometimes confused with each other. In each case, one of the set takes an object and the other doesn't, and each member of the set has a somewhat different meaning:

Lie (recline)	She <u>lies</u> in bed all day. *(present)*
	She <u>lay</u> in bed all last week. *(past)*
Lay (put)	He <u>lays</u> his dishes on the table. *(present)*
	He <u>laid</u> his dishes on the table. *(past)*
Sit (be seated)	Please <u>sit</u> here by the window. *(present)*
	He <u>sat</u> by the window in class. *(past)*
Set (put)	Please <u>set</u> the flowers on the table. *(present)*
	He <u>set</u> the flowers on the chair before he left. *(past)*
Rise (get up)	They all <u>rise</u> early in the morning. *(present)*
	They all <u>rose</u> early yesterday too. *(past)*
Raise (lift up)	Can you <u>raise</u> that weight above your head? *(present)*
	He <u>raised</u> the curtain for the play. *(past)*

Verb tense

The four verb tenses for present, past, and future are as follows:

- Simple:

  I see   I saw   I will see

- Progressive: "be" + *–ing* form of the verb

  I am seeing   I was seeing   I will be seeing

- Perfect: "have," "had," or "shall" + the *–ed* form of the verb

  I have walked   I had walked   I will have walked

- Perfect progressive: "have" or "had" + "been" + *–ing* form of the verb

I have been singing	I had been singing	I will have been singing

  (For a guide to using the tenses, see section 30a.)

hint

Verb Endings

Avoid the verb ending problem that omits the final "d" or uses "of" instead of "have" in such forms as the following:

might have <u>like</u> to (should be: might have <u>liked</u> to)

could <u>of</u> (should be: could <u>have</u>)

<u>suppose</u> to (should be: <u>supposed</u> to)

Verb voice

Verb voice tells whether the verb is in the active or passive voice. In the active voice, the subject **performs** the action of the verb. In the passive voice, the subject **receives** the action. The doer of the action in the passive voice may be omitted or may appear in a "by the . . . " phrase.

Active: The child sang the song.

Passive: The song was sung by the child.

Verb mood

The mood of a verb tells whether it expresses a fact or opinion (**indicative** mood); expresses a command, request, or advice (**imperative** mood); or expresses a doubt, wish, recommendation, or something contrary to fact (**subjunctive** mood).

Indicative: The new software <u>runs</u> well on this computer.

Imperative: <u>Watch</u> for falling rock.

Subjunctive: In the subjunctive, present tense verbs stay in the simple base form and do not indicate the number and person of the subject. Use the subjunctive mood in "that" clauses following verbs such as "ask," "insist," and "request."

In the past tense, the same form as simple past is used; however, for the verb "be," "were" is used for all persons and numbers.

It is important that he <u>join</u> the committee.

He insisted that she <u>be</u> one of the leaders of the group.

If I <u>were</u> you, I wouldn't ask that question.

14

Pronouns

14a   Pronoun case

Pronouns, the words that substitute for nouns, change case according to their use in a sentence.

Subject: <u>He</u> bought some film. It is <u>he</u>.
Object: Deatrise gave <u>him</u> the film.
Possessive: No one used <u>his</u> film.

Pronoun Case

	Subject		Object		Possessive	
	Sing.	Pl.	Sing.	Pl.	Sing.	Pl.
1st person	I	we	me	us	my	our
					mine	ours
2nd person	you	you	you	you	your	your
					yours	yours
3rd person	he	they	him	them	his	their
						theirs
	she	they	her	them	her	their
					hers	theirs
	it	they	it	them	it, its	their
						theirs

hint

Common Problems with Pronouns

HINT 1

Remember that "between," "except," and "with" are prepositions, and they take pronouns in the object case:

between you and me   (*not:* between you and I)

except Amit and her   (*not:* except Amit and she)

HINT 2

Possessive case pronouns never take apostrophes:

his shoes   (*not:* his' shoes)

its eye   (*not:* it's eye)

HINT 3

Don't use "them" as a pointing pronoun in place of "those" or "these." Use "them" only as the object by itself.

those pages   (*not:* them pages)

HINT 4

Use possessive case before *–ing* verb forms.

They applauded his scoring a goal. (*not:* him scoring)

HINT 5

Reflexive pronouns are those that end in *–self* or *–selves* and are used to intensify the nouns they refer back to:

I soaked myself in suntan oil.

Please help yourself.

Don't use the reflexive pronoun in other cases because it sounds as if it might be more correct. (It isn't.)

I

Joseph and ~~myself~~ went to pick up the tickets.
^

me

They included ~~myself~~ in the group.
^

Pronoun case in compound constructions

To find the right case when your sentence has two pronouns or a noun and a pronoun, temporarily eliminate the noun or one of the pronouns as you read the sentence to yourself. You will hear the case that is needed.

Which is correct?   Nathan and him ordered a pizza.
                         (or)
                    Nathan and he ordered a pizza.

Test: Would you say "Him ordered a pizza"?
                    The correct pronoun here is "he."

Which is correct?   I gave those tickets to Mikki and she.
                         (or)
                    I gave those tickets to Mikki and her.

Test: Would you say, "I gave those tickets to she"?
                    When in doubt, some writers mistakenly choose the subject case, thinking it sounds more formal. But the correct pronoun here is "her," the object case, because it is the object of the preposition "to."

"Who/whom"

In informal speech, some writers do not distinguish between "who" and "whom." But for formal writing, the cases are as follows:

Subject	Object	Possessive
who	whom	whose
whoever	whomever	

Subject: <u>Who</u> is going to drive that van?
Object: To <u>whom</u> should I give this booklet?
Possessive: Everyone wondered <u>whose</u> coat that was.

---

hint
Using "Who" and "Whom"

If you aren't sure whether to use "who" or "whom," turn a question into a statement or rearrange the order of the phrase:

Question: (Who, Whom) are you looking for?
Statement: You are looking for whom.

(continued)

Sentence:	She is someone (who,whom) I have already met.
Rearranged order:	I have already met whom.
Correct sentence:	She is someone whom I have already met.

Pronoun case after "than" or "as"

In comparisons using "than" or "as," choose the correct pronoun case by recalling the words that are omitted:

He is taller than (I, me). (The omitted words are "am tall.")
He is taller than <u>I</u> (am tall).

My sister likes her cat more than (I, me). (The omitted words here are "she likes.")
My sister likes her cat more than (she likes) <u>me</u>.

"We" or "us" before nouns

When combining "we" or "us" with a noun, such as "we players," use the case that is appropriate for the noun. You can hear that by omitting the noun and seeing which sounds correct.

(We, Us) players chose to pay for our own equipment.

Test: Would you say "Us chose to pay for our own equipment"? The correct pronoun here is "We."

---

hint

"We" or "Us"

Remember the famous opening words of the U.S. Declaration of Independence: "<u>We</u> the people. . . . "

Pronoun case with infinitives ("to" + verb)

When using pronouns after infinitives, verb forms with "to" + verb, use the object case. (You can also hear this by omitting a noun that may precede the pronoun.)

She offered to drive Orin and (I, me) to the meeting.

Test: Would you say, "She offered to drive I to
                   the meeting"? The correct pronoun here
                   is "me."

Pronoun case before gerunds (*–ing* verb forms)

If a pronoun is used to modify a gerund (an *–ing* word), use
the possessive case.

> She was proud of (us, our) walking in the fund-raising
> marathon.

> The correct form here is the possessive, "our."

14b Pronoun antecedents

Pronouns substitute for nouns. In the sentence "Emilio
washed his car," the pronoun "his" is a substitute for the
noun "Emilio" (to avoid unnecessary repetition) and refers
back to Emilio. The noun that a pronoun refers back to is
its antecedent. For clarity, then, pronouns should agree in
number and gender with their antecedents. (In the sentences "Emilio washed their car" or "Emilio washed her
car," you would assume there is a different car being
referred to.)

Singular: The <u>student</u> turned in <u>her</u> lab report.

Plural: The <u>students</u> turned in <u>their</u> lab reports.

Indefinite pronouns

Indefinite pronouns are those pronouns that don't refer to
any specific person or thing such as "anyone," "no one,"
"someone," "something," "everybody," "none," and "each."
Some of them may seem to have a plural meaning, but in formal writing, treat them as singular. Others, such as "many,"
are always plural, and some can be singular or plural
depending on the meaning of the sentence.

   When using indefinite pronouns that are normally treated
as singular, some writers prefer to use the plural to avoid
sexist language (section 10). But as an alternative, you can
use "his or her" (which can be wordy) or switch to plural.

> <u>Everyone</u> in the class took out <u>his</u> notebook.

> <u>Everyone</u> in the class took out <u>his or her</u> notebook.

> The <u>students</u> took out <u>their</u> notebooks.

Collective nouns

When you use collective nouns such as "committee," "family," "group," and "audience," treat them as singular because they are acting as a group.

The <u>jury</u> handed in <u>its</u> verdict.

Generic or general nouns

When you use generic nouns to indicate members of a group, such as "voter," "student," and "doctor," treat them as singular. To avoid sexist language, switch to plural.

A truck <u>driver</u> should keep <u>his</u> road maps close at hand.

Truck <u>drivers</u> should keep <u>their</u> road maps close at hand.

14c   Pronoun reference

To avoid reader confusion, be sure that your pronouns have a clear reference to their antecedents. There are several possible problems to avoid:

Ambiguous pronoun reference

When a pronoun does not clearly indicate which of two or more possible antecedents it refers to, the reference is ambiguous. Rewrite the sentence to make sure the reference is clear.

Unclear reference: Marina told Michelle that she took <u>her</u> bike to the library.

her = Marina?   her = Michelle?

(Did Marina take Michelle's bike to the library, or did Marina take her own bike to the library?)

Clear reference: When Marina took Michelle's bike to the library, she told Michelle she was borrowing it.

Vague pronoun reference ("this," "that," and "which")

When you use "this," "that," and "which" to refer to something, be sure that the word refers to a specific antecedent that has been named.

Vague pronoun reference: Ray worked in a national forest last summer, and <u>this</u> may be his career choice.

this = ?

(What does "this" refer to? Because no word or phrase in the first part of the sentence refers to the pronoun, the sentence needs to be revised so that the antecedent is stated.)

Clear pronoun reference: Ray worked in a national forest last summer, and <u>working as a forest ranger</u> may be his career choice.

Indefinite use of "you," "it," and "they"

Avoid the use of "you," "it," and "they" when they don't refer to any specific group.

Vague pronoun reference: Everyone knows <u>you</u> should use sunscreen lotion when out in bright summer sun.

you = ?

Clear pronoun reference: It is well known that <u>people</u> should use sunscreen lotion when out in bright summer sun.

Vague pronoun reference: In Hollywood <u>they</u> don't know what type of movies the American public wants to see.

they = ?

Clear pronoun reference: In Hollywood, <u>screenwriters and producers</u> don't know what type of movies the American public wants to see.

15

Adjectives and Adverbs

Adjectives and adverbs are modifiers, but they modify different kinds of words:

Adjectives
- modify nouns and pronouns
- answer the questions "which?" "how many?" and "what kind?"

<u>six</u> packages (how many? <u>six</u>)
<u>cheerful</u> smile (what kind? <u>cheerful</u>)

It is <u>cold</u>.

(An adjective after a linking verb modifies the subject and is called a "subject complement." Here, "cold" is an adjective modifying the subject pronoun "it.")

The water tastes <u>salty</u>. water = salty

(Some verbs, such as "taste," "feel," "appear," and "smell," can be linking verbs.)

Adverbs
- modify verbs, verb forms, adjectives, and other adverbs
- answer the questions "how?" "when?" "where?" and "to what extent?"
- Most (but not all) adverbs end in *–ly*

danced <u>gracefully</u> (how? <u>gracefully</u>)

<u>very</u> long string (how long? <u>very</u> long)

He ran ~~quick~~ quickly. (How did he run? <u>quickly</u>)

They sing ~~real~~ really loud. (How loud? <u>really</u>)

Adjectives	Adverbs
sure	surely
real	really
good	well
bad	badly

"Good," "bad," "badly," and "well"

The modifiers "good," "bad," "badly," and "well" can cause problems because they are occasionally misused in speech. In addition, "well" can function as an adjective or an adverb.

well (adjective) = healthy   well (adverb) = done satisfactorily

He played <u>well</u>. (*not:* good)

Despite the surgery, I feel <u>well</u>. (*not:* good)

The linebacker played <u>badly</u> today. (*not:* bad)

She feels <u>bad</u> about missing that meeting. (*not:* badly)

He looked <u>good</u> in that suit. (*not:* well)

hint

Completing Comparisons

When you use adverbs such as "so," "such," and "too," be sure to complete the phrase or clause.

that she laughed out loud

She is so happy.
  ^

to ask for help

Tran's problem is that he is too proud.
  ^

Comparatives and superlatives

Adjectives and adverbs are often used to show comparison, and the degree of comparison is indicated in their forms. Adjectives and adverbs with one or two syllables add *–er* and *–est* as endings, and longer adjectives and adverbs combine with the words "more" and "most" or "less" and "least."

- Positive (when no comparison is made):

  a <u>large</u> box   a <u>cheerful</u> smile

- Comparative (when two things are compared):

  the <u>larger</u> of the two boxes   a <u>more cheerful</u> smile

- Superlative (when three or more things are compared):

  the <u>largest</u> box   the <u>most cheerful</u> smile

Regular Forms of Comparison

Positive	Comparative	Superlative
(for one)	(for two)	(for three or more)
tall	taller	tallest
pretty	prettier	prettiest
selfish	more selfish	most selfish
unusual	more unusual	most unusual

Irregular Forms of Comparison

Positive	Comparative	Superlative
(for one)	(for two)	(for three or more)
good	better	best
well	better	best
little	less	least
some	more	most
much	more	most
many	more	most
bad, badly	worse	worst

Absolute adjectives and adverbs

Some adjectives and adverbs such as "unique," "perfect," and "final" cannot logically be compared because there can't be degrees of being final or unique or perfect.

Terri has a ~~most~~ unique smile.
It was a ~~most~~ perfect evening.

16

Modifiers

16a   Dangling modifiers

A dangling modifier is a word or group of words that refers to (or modifies) a word or phrase that has not been clearly stated in the sentence. When an introductory phrase does not name the doer of the action, the phrase is assumed to refer to the subject of the independent clause that follows.

Having finished the assignment, Serkan turned on the TV.

("Serkan," the subject of the independent clause, is the doer of the action in the introductory phrase.)

However, when the intended subject (or doer of the action) of the introductory phrase is not stated, the result is a dangling modifier.

Having finished the assignment, the TV was turned on.

(This sentence is not logical because it implies that the TV finished the homework.)

Dangling modifiers most frequently occur at the beginning of the sentence but can also appear at the end. They often have an *–ing* verb or a "to" + verb phrase near the start of the phrase. To repair a dangling modifier, name the subject in the dangling phrase or as the subject of the sentence.

Dangling: After completing a degree in education, more experience in the classroom is also needed to prepare a good teacher.

Revised: After completing a degree in education, good teachers also need to gain more experience in the classroom.

Dangling: To work as a lifeguard, practice in CPR is required.

Revised: To work as a lifeguard, applicants are required to have practice in CPR.

Dangling: After a long conversation on her cell phone, its battery needed recharging.

(This sentence implies that the cell phone battery had a long conversation.)

Revised: After a long conversation on her cell phone, she needed to recharge its battery.

16b   Misplaced modifiers

Misplaced modifiers are words or groups of words placed so far away from what is being referred to that the reader may be confused.

Misplaced modifier: The assembly line workers were told that they had been fired <u>by the personnel director</u>.

(Were the workers told by the personnel director that they had been fired? Or were they told by someone else that the personnel director had fired them?)

Revised: The assembly line workers were told by the personnel director that they had been fired.

Misplaced modifiers are often the source of comedians' humor, as in the classic often used by Groucho Marx and others:

The other day I shot an elephant in my pajamas. How he got in my pajamas I'll never know.

Single-word modifiers such as "only," "even," and "hardly" should be placed immediately before the words they modify or as close to that word as possible. Note the difference in meaning in these two sentences:

I earned nearly $50. (The amount was almost $50, but not quite.)

I nearly earned $50. (I almost had the opportunity to earn $50, but it didn't work out.)

---

hint

Placing Modifiers Correctly

Some one-word modifiers that may get misplaced:

almost	hardly	merely	only
even	just	nearly	simply

16c Split infinitives

Split infinitives occur when modifiers are inserted between "to" and the verb. Some people object to split infinitives, but others consider them grammatically acceptable when other phrasing would be less natural.

to <u>quickly</u> go

(Some people consider this a split infinitive that can easily be revised to "to go quickly.")

to <u>easily</u> reach

(Here "easily" fits naturally between the "to" and the verb "reach." Most writers find this preferable to a sentence such as "He wanted easily to reach the top shelf.")

Some split infinitives such as "to more than double" are almost impossible to rephrase so that there is no modifier between "to" and the verb.

17

Shifts

To maintain consistency in writing, use the same perspective throughout a paper by maintaining the same person: first person ("I"), second person ("you"), and third person ("he," "she," "it," "one," or "they"). Maintain consistency in number, tense, and tone also.

Unnecessary shift in person:	In a <u>person's</u> life, the most important *(3rd person)* thing <u>you</u> do is to decide on a career. *(2nd person)*
Revised:	In a <u>person's</u> life, the most important thing <u>he</u> or <u>she</u> does is to decide on a career.

Unnecessary shift in number:	The working <u>woman</u> faces many
	(singular)
	challenges to advancement. When <u>they</u>
	(plural)
	marry and have children, <u>she</u> may need to
	(singular)
	take a leave of absence.
Revised:	Working <u>women</u> face many challenges to advancement. When <u>they</u> marry and have children, <u>they</u> may need to take a leave of absence.

Keep writing with verbs in the same time (past, present, or future) in your verbs unless the logic of what you are writing about requires a switch.

Unnecessary shift in tense:	While we <u>were watching</u> the last
	(past)
	game of the World Series, the picture suddenly <u>gets</u> fuzzy.
	(present)
Revised:	While we <u>were watching</u> the last game of the World Series, the picture suddenly <u>got</u> fuzzy.

Once you choose a formal or informal tone for a paper, keep that tone consistent in your word choices. A sudden intrusion of a very formal word or phrase in an informal narrative or the use of slang or informal words in a formal report or essay indicates the writer's loss of control over tone.

Unnecessary shift in tone:	The responsibility of the welfare worker is to assist a family's struggle to obtain funds for the <u>kids'</u> clothing and food.

("Kids" is a very informal word choice here for a sentence that is somewhat formal in tone.)

Revised:	The responsibility of the welfare worker is to assist in a family's struggle to obtain funds for the <u>children's</u> clothing and food.

IV
Punctuation

. . . .

Contents of this section

QUESTION AND CORRECT

	SECTION	PAGE

18

Sentence Punctuation Patterns (for Commas, Semicolons, and Colons)

There are nine patterns to choose from when you use commas, semicolons, and colons in sentences. The patterns to use depend on whether you are writing a simple, compound, or complex sentence (see the Glossary of Grammatical Terms):

- For simple sentences, use patterns 1 and 5.

- For compound sentences, use patterns 2, 3, 4, and 6.

- For complex sentences, use patterns 7, 8, and 9.

1. (Independent clause).

   Everyone agreed with her suggestion.

2. (Independent clause), *and* (independent clause).

   > *but*
   > *for*
   > *or*
   > *nor*
   > *so*
   > *yet*

   (the coordinating conjunctions)

   It took four years for the tree to produce a crop, **but** the fruit was abundant.

3. (Independent clause); (independent clause).

   They arrived late; they offered no excuse.

4. (Independent clause); **thus**, (independent clause).

   > *however,*
   > *nevertheless,*

   (or other independent clause markers)

   They arrived late; **however**, they offered no excuse.

5. (Independent clause): (example, list of items, or explanation).

> They needed three items: a contract, her signature, and payment.

> He had only one fault: stupidity.

6. (Independent clause): (independent clause).

> The candidate promised fewer taxes: he campaigned on a platform of eliminating property taxes.

7. **If** (dependent clause), (independent clause).

After
Because
Since
When

(or other dependent clause markers)

> **If** he studies more, his grades will improve.
>   (or)
(Independent clause) **if** (dependent clause).

because
since
when
after

> His grades will improve **if** he studies more.

8. Subject, (nonessential dependent clause), (verb/predicate).

> Mako, who is my cousin, is going to major in economics.

9. Subject (essential dependent clause) (verb/predicate).

> The movie that I rented last night was a box office failure.

19

Commas

19a   Commas between independent clauses

To use commas in independent clauses, you need to know the following:

Independent clause:	a clause that can stand alone as a sentence
Compound sentence:	a sentence with two or more independent clauses

When you join two or more independent clauses to make a compound sentence, use a comma and any of the seven joining words (coordinating conjunctions) listed below. Place a comma before the joining word. A compound sentence that does not have both the comma and the joining word is called a "comma splice" or "run-on." (See section 12.)

The seven joining words

F or
A nd
N or   Vanilla is my favorite ice cream, but chocolate is
B ut   a close second.
O r
Y et
S o

(Some writers remember this list as "FAN BOYS," spelled out by the first letters of each word.)

Alternative:	If the two independent clauses are very short, some writers leave out the comma.

It started raining but the game continued.

Alternative:	If one of the independent clauses has a comma in it, use a semicolon instead as part of the joining pair.

Katie, not Alesha, is captain of the team; **but** Alesha assists the coach during practices.

19b   Commas after introductory word groups

If you include introductory words, phrases, or clauses before the main part of your sentence, place a comma after the introductory part to indicate the break.

Word:	However, the farmer switched his crop to hay.
Phrase:	Having lived in Korea, he enjoyed eating kim chee.
Clause:	While I was working on my car, it started to rain.
Alternative:	If the introductory element is short (no more than four or five words) and not likely to cause confusion, some writers leave out the comma. In the second example below, some readers might, at first, misread the sentence as stating that Matt was eating the cat, so a comma is needed there.

In most cases the statistics were reliable.
While Matt ate, the cat watched intently.

19c   Commas before and after nonessential elements

When you include words, phrases, or clauses that are not essential to the meaning of the sentence and could be included in another sentence instead, place commas before and after the nonessential element.

Dr. Gupta, who is a cardiac surgeon, retired after fifty years of practice.

Essential and Nonessential Clauses

You can decide if an element is essential by reading the sentence without it. If the meaning changes, that element is essential.

ESSENTIAL:

Apples <u>that are green</u> are usually very tart.

If you remove the clause "that are green," the statement changes to indicate that all apples are usually very tart.

(continued)

NONESSENTIAL:

Mangos, <u>which are Megan's favorite fruit</u>, are on sale this week at the market.

Whether or not mangos are Megan's favorite fruit, they are still on sale this week at the market. Thus "<u>which are Megan's favorite fruit</u>" is a nonessential element.

19d   Commas in series and lists

Use commas when you have three or more items in a series or list.

The painting was done in blues, greens, and reds.

Wherever Mr. Chaugh went in the town, whatever he saw, and whomever he met, he was reminded of his childhood days there.

Alternative: Although most writers prefer to use the comma before "and" in a list of three of more items, some writers omit it.

The menu included omelets, pastas and salads.

---

hint

Commas with Lists

Remember that there must be at least three items in a list in order to use commas. Some writers mistakenly put a comma between two items (often verbs) in a sentence.

Misused comma: No one had ever been able to locate the source of the river/and follow all its tributaries.

Revised: No one had ever been able to locate the source of the river and follow all its tributaries.

19e   Commas with adjectives

When you include two or more adjectives that describe a noun equally, separate the adjectives by commas. But not all adjectives describe a noun equally. A quick test to see if the adjectives are equal is to switch the order. If that still sounds correct to your ear, they're equal. Another test is to insert "and" between the adjectives.

happy, healthy child

(You can switch this to "healthy, happy child." You can also write "happy and healthy child.")

six large dogs

(You cannot switch this to "large six dogs" or "six and large dogs.")

19f Commas with interrupting words or phrases

Use commas to set off words and phrases that interrupt the sentence.

Louisa Marcos, a math teacher, won the award.

The committee was, however, unable to agree.

The weather prediction, much to our surprise, was accurate.

19g Commas with dates, addresses, geographical names, and numbers

- With dates
    In a heading or list:

    February 25, 2005 (or) 25 February, 2005

    (No commas are needed to separate the day and month if the day is placed before the month.)

    In a sentence:

    The order was shipped on March 9, 2004, and not received until January 18, 2005.

- With addresses
    In a letter heading or on an envelope:

    Michael Cavanaugh, Jr.
    1404 Danton Drive
    Mineola, New Mexico 43723

In a sentence:

If you need more information, write to General Investment, 132 Maple Avenue, Martinsville, IL 60122.

- With geographical names
  Put a comma after each item in a place name.

  The conference next year will be in Chicago, Illinois, and in New Orleans, Louisiana, the year after that.

- With numbers

  8,190,434 27,000   1,300 (or) 1300
  The herd included 9,200 head of cattle.

19h   Commas with quotations

Use a comma after expressions such as "he said."

Everyone was relieved when the chairperson said, "I will table this motion until the next meeting."

19i   Unnecessary commas

- Don't separate a subject from its verb.

Unnecessary: Increasing numbers of eighteen-year-olds who vote are calling for stricter laws.

- Don't put a comma between two verbs.

Unnecessary: We offered to lend her our notes and help her with the homework.

- Don't put a comma before every "and" or "but."

Unnecessary: The automobile industry now designs fuel-efficient cars and is finding a large market for them.

- Don't put a comma before a direct object, especially a clause that starts with "that."

Unnecessary: Shaundra explained to me that she was interested in hearing my view.

- Don't put a comma before a dependent clause when it comes after an independent clause, except for extreme contrast.

Unnecessary: Deer populations are exploding, because their natural enemies are disappearing.

But: He was delighted with the news, although he needed some time to absorb it.

- Don't put a comma after "such as" or "especially."

Unnecessary: The take-out shop sold various soups, such as minestrone, bean, and chicken noodle.

20

Apostrophes

20a   Apostrophes with possessives

The apostrophe indicates a form of ownership, but this is not always obvious. To test for possession, turn the two words around into an "of the" phrase.

Manuel's skates   day's pay
the skates of Manuel   the pay of the day

- For singular nouns, use 's:

book 's cover   river 's edge

- For singular nouns ending in –s, the –s after the apostrophe is optional if adding that –s makes the pronunciation difficult.

James 's coat   (or)   James' coat
Mr. Mendozes' coat   grass 's color

- For plural nouns ending in –s, add an apostrophe.

books' covers   rivers' edges

- For plural nouns that do not end in –*s*, use *'s*.

  children**'s** toys   oxen**'s** tails

- For possession with two or more nouns:

When jointly owned: Jim and Sabrina**'s** house

  (The house belongs jointly to both Jim and Sabrina.)

When individually owned: Jim**'s** and Sabrina**'s** plans

  (Jim and Sabrina each have their own plans.)

- For compound nouns:

  sister-in-law**'s** car   secretary of state**'s** office

- For indefinite pronouns (someone, everybody, etc.), use *'s*.

  no one**'s** fault   somebody**'s** hat

---

hint

Using Apostrophes

When you aren't sure where the apostrophe goes, follow this order. Notice that everything to the left of the apostrophe is the word and its plural. Everything after the plural is the possessive marker.

1. First write the word.
2. Put in the plural if needed.
3. Then put in the apostrophe for possession.

	Word	Plural	Possessive Marker
girl's glove	girl		's
girls' gloves	girl	s	'
men's gloves	men		's

20b   Apostrophes with contractions

Use the apostrophe to mark the omitted letter or letters in contractions.

  it's = it is   don't = do not   they're = they are
  o'clock = of the clock   '89 = 1989

20c   Apostrophes with plurals

Use the apostrophe to form the plurals of letters, abbreviations with periods, numbers, and words used as words.

She got all A's last semester.

They all have Ph.D.'s.

He picked all 5's in the lottery.

Melissa's "maybe's" were irritating.

Alternative: For some writers, the apostrophe is optional if the plural is clear.

| 9s | (or) | 9's |
| 1960s | (or) | 1960's |

But the apostrophe is needed here:

a's   A's

(Without the apostrophe, these might be the word "as.")

20d   Unnecessary apostrophes

- Don't use an apostrophe with possessive pronouns (*"his"*, *"hers"*, *"its"*, *"yours"*, *"whose"*, etc.).

Not correct: his' arm   it's edge   yours'
Revised: his arm   its edge   yours

- Don't use an apostrophe with regular forms of plurals that do not show possession.

Not correct: The apple's were ripe.   They reduced the prices'.
Revised: The apples were ripe.   They reduced the prices.

21

Semicolons

The semicolon is a stronger mark of punctuation than the comma, and it is used with two kinds of closely related elements:

1. between independent clauses
2. between items in a series

It is almost like a period but does not come at the end of the sentence.

21a   Semicolons to separate independent clauses

Use a semicolon when joining two independent clauses not joined by the seven connectors that require a comma: *"and," "but," "for," "or," "nor," "so",* and *"yet."*

Two patterns for using semicolons:

1. independent clause **+ semicolon** + independent clause

    The television shots showed extensive flood damage; houses were drifting downriver.

2. independent clause **+ semicolon + joining word + comma** + independent clause

    There was no warning before the flood; **however**, no lives were lost.

Some frequently used joining words:

also,	finally,	instead,
besides,	for example,	on the contrary,
consequently,	however,	still,
even so,	in addition,	therefore,

Alternative: You can use a semicolon between two independent clauses joined with a coordinating conjunction (section 19a) when one of those clauses has its own comma. The semicolon makes the break between the two clauses clearer.

The police officer, who was the first person on the scene, wrote down the information; and the newspaper relied on his account of the accident.

21b   Semicolons in a series

Normally, commas are used between three or more items in a series (page 71), but when each item has its own comma, a semicolon can be used between items for clarity.

Hannah, Carmencita, and Heidi
(or)
Hannah, my first cousin; Carmencita, my best friend; and Heidi, my neighbor

21c   Semicolons with quotation marks

If a semicolon is needed, put it after the quotation marks.

Her answer to every question was, "I'll think about that";
she wasn't ready to make a decision.

21d   Unnecessary semicolons

- Don't use a semicolon between a clause and a phrase.

  Mexico is my favorite vacation place; especially the

  (should be a comma)

  beaches in Cancun.

- Don't use a semicolon in place of a dash, comma, or colon.

  She spent the funds on a necessary piece of equipment for
  her home office; a computer.

  (should be a colon)

22

Quotation Marks

22a   Quotation marks with direct quotations of prose, poetry, and dialogue

When you are writing the exact words you've seen in print or
heard, use quotation marks when the quotation is less than
four lines. For quotations that are four lines or longer, indent
with no quotation marks.

Mrs. Alphonse said, "The test scores show improved
reading ability."

In his poem, "Mending Wall," Robert Frost says:
"Something there is that doesn't love a wall, / That sends
the frozen-ground-swell under it."

(Notice the use of the slash to separate the two lines of poetry here.)

In his poem, "Mending Wall," Robert Frost questions the building of barriers and walls:

> Something there is that doesn't love a wall,
>
> That sends the frozen-ground-swell under it,
>
> And spills the upper boulders in the sun;
>
> And makes gaps even two can pass abreast.

- If you have a quotation within a quotation, use single quotation marks (') to set off the quotation enclosed inside the longer quotation.

  The newspaper reporter explained: "When I interviewed the lawyer, he said, 'No comment.' "

- If you leave words out of a quotation, use an ellipsis mark (three periods, see page 86) to indicate the missing words.

  The lawyer stated that he "would not . . . under any circumstances violate the client's desire for privacy."

- If you add material within a quotation, use brackets [ ] (see section 23g).

  No one, explained the scientist, "could duplicate [Mineffsky's] experiment without having his notes."

- If you quote dialogue, write each person's speech as a separate paragraph. Closely related bits of narrative can be included with a paragraph with dialogue. If one person's speech goes on for several paragraphs, use quotation marks at the beginning of each paragraph, but not at the end of all paragraphs before the last one. To signal the end of the person's speech, put quotation marks at the end of the last paragraph.

22b Quotation marks for minor titles and parts of wholes

Use quotation marks for titles of parts of larger works (titles of book chapters, magazine articles, and episodes of television and radio series) and for short minor works (songs, short stories, essays, short poems, one-act plays). Do not use quotation marks when referring to the Bible or legal documents. For larger, more complete works, use italics (see section 25a).

> "The Star Spangled Banner"   Exodus 2:1
> "Think Warm Thoughts" (an episode on *ER*)

22c Quotation marks for words

Use quotation marks (or italics) for words that are used as words rather than for their meaning.

> It was tiresome to hear her always inserting "cool" or "you know" in each sentence she spoke.

22d Use of other punctuation with quotation marks

- Place commas and periods inside quotation marks. However, in MLA format, when you include a page reference, put the period after the page reference.

  > . . . was an advantage," she said.

  > . . . until tomorrow."

  > . . . when the eclipse occurs" (9).

- Place colons and semicolons outside the quotation marks.

  > . . . until tomorrow":   Moreover, this is done"; . . . .

- Place the dash, exclamation mark, and question mark before the end set of quotation marks when the punctuation mark applies to the quotation. When the punctuation mark does not apply to the quotation, put the punctuation after the end set of quotation marks.

  > He asked, "Should I return the book to her?"

  > "Should I return the book to her?" he asked.

  > Did Professor Sandifur really say, "No class tomorrow"?

22e Unnecessary quotation marks

Don't use quotation marks around titles of your essays, common nicknames, bits of humor, technical terms, and trite or well-known expressions.

> "Bubba" wanted the fastest "modem" available.

23

Other Punctuation

23a Hyphens

Hyphens have a variety of uses:

- For compound words:
  Some compound words are one word:

  weekend   mastermind   granddaughter   homepage

  Some compound words are two words:

  high school   executive director   turn off

  Some compound words are joined by hyphens:

  father-in-law   president-elect   clear-cut

  Fractions and numbers from twenty-one to ninety-nine that are spelled out have hyphens.

  one-half   thirty-six   nine-tenths

  Particularly for new words or compounds that you are forming, check your dictionary. You may find an answer there, but not all hyphenated words appear there yet, especially new ones. Also, you will find that usage varies between dictionaries for some compounds.

  e-mail (or) email   witch-hunt (or) witch hunt

  wave-length (or) wavelength (or) wave length

  For hyphenated words in a series, use hyphens as follows:

  four-, five-, and six-page essays

- For two-word units:
  Use a hyphen when two or more words placed before a noun work together as a single unit to describe the noun. When these words come after the noun, they are usually not hyphenated. But don't use hyphens with adverbs such as –*ly* modifiers.

  He needed up-to-date statistics. (or) He needed statistics that were up to date.

  They repaired the six-inch pipe. (or) They repaired the pipe that was six inches long.

(but not with adverbs such as those ending in –*ly*) That was a widely known fact.

- For prefixes, suffixes, and letters joined to a word:
  Use hyphens between words and prefixes *self–, all–,* and *ex–.*

  self-contained   all-American   ex-president

  For other prefixes, such as *anti–, pro–,* and *co–,* use the dictionary as a guide.

  co-author   antibacterial   pro-choice

  Use a hyphen when joining a prefix to a capitalized word or to figures and numbers.

  anti-American   non-Catholic   pre-1998

  Use a hyphen when you add the suffix *–elect.*

  president-elect

  Use a hyphen to avoid doubling vowels and tripling consonants and to avoid ambiguity.

  anti-intellectual   bell-like   re-cover   re-creation

- To divide words between syllables when the last part of the word appears on the next line.

  Every spring the nation's capitol is flooded with tourists snapping pictures of the cherry blossoms.

  When dividing words at the end of a line:

- Don't divide one-syllable words.

- Don't leave one or two letters at the end of a line.

- Don't put fewer than three letters on the next line.

- Don't divide the last word in a paragraph or the last word on a page.

- Divide compound words so that the hyphen for the compound comes at the end of the line. Or put the whole compound word on the next line.

23b Colons

Use colons as follows:

- To announce elements at the end of the sentence

  The company sold only electronics they could service: computers, stereos, CD players, and television sets.

- To separate independent clauses
  Use a colon instead of a semicolon to separate two independent clauses when the second restates or amplifies the first.

  The town council voted not to pave the gravel roads outside of town: they did not have the funds for road improvement.

- To announce long quotations
  Use a colon to announce a long quotation (more than one sentence) or a quotation not introduced by words such as "said," "remarked," or "stated."

  The candidate for office offered only one reason to vote for her: "I will not raise parking meter rates."

- In salutations and between elements

  Dear Dr. Philippa: 6:12 a.m.
  Genesis 1:8   scale of 1:3
  Maryland: My Home   Chicago: Howe Books

- With quotation marks
  If a colon is needed, put it after the closing quotation mark.

  "One sign of intelligence is not arguing with your boss": that was her motto for office harmony.

- Unnecessary colons
  Do not use a colon after a verb or phrases like "such as" or "consisted of."

Not correct: The two most valuable players were: Timon Lasmon and Maynor Field.

Revised: The two most valuable players were Timon Lasmon and Maynor Field.

Not correct: The camping equipment consisted of: tents, bug spray, lanterns, matches, and dehydrated food.

Revised: The camping equipment consisted of tents, bug spray, lanterns, matches, and dehydrated food.

23c   End punctuation

Periods

Use a period at the end of a sentence that is a statement, mild command, indirect question, or polite question where an answer isn't expected.

Electric cars are growing in popularity. (statement)

Do not use your calculator during the test. (mild command)

Would you please let me know when you're done. (polite question)

Use a period with abbreviations, but don't use a second period if the abbreviation is at the end of the sentence.

R.S.V.P.   U.S.A.   Dr.   Mr.   8 a.m.

A period is not needed after agencies, common abbreviations, names of well-known companies, and state abbreviations used by the U.S. Postal Service.

NATO   NBA   CIA   YMCA   IBM   DNA   TX

Put periods that follow quotations inside the quotation mark. But if there is a reference to a source, put the period after the reference.

She said, "I'm going to Alaska next week."

Neman notes "the claim is unfounded" (6).

Question marks

Use a question mark after a direct question but not after an indirect one.

Did anyone see my laptop computer? (direct question)

Jules wonders if he should buy a new stereo. (indirect question)

Place a question mark inside the quotation marks if the quotation is a question. Place the question mark outside the quotation marks if the whole sentence is a question.

Drora asked, "Is she on time?"

Did Eli really say, "I'm in love"?

Question marks may be used between parts of a series.

Would you like to see a movie? go shopping? eat at a restaurant?

Use a question mark to indicate doubt about the correctness of the preceding date, number, or other piece of information. But do not use it to indicate sarcasm.

The ship landed in Greenland about 1521 (?) but did not keep a record of where it was.

Not correct: Matti's sense of humor (?) evaded me.

Revised: Matti's sense of humor evaded me.

Exclamation marks

- Use the exclamation mark after a strong command or a statement said with great emphasis or with strong feeling. But do not overuse the exclamation mark.

  I'm absolutely delighted!

Unnecessary: Wow! What a great party! I enjoyed every minute of it!

- Enclose the exclamation mark within the quotation marks only if it belongs to the quotation.

  He threw open the door and exclaimed, "I've won the lottery!"

23d   Dashes

The dash is somewhat informal but can be used to add emphasis or clarity, to mark an interruption or shift in tone, or to introduce a list. Use two hyphens to indicate the dash when you are typing, and do not leave a space before or after the hyphen.

To be a millionaire, the owner of a yacht, and a race car driver—this was his goal.

The cat looked at me so sweetly—with a dead rat in its mouth.

23e   Slashes

Use the slash to mark the end of a line of poetry and to indicate acceptable alternatives. For poetry, leave a space before and after the slash. For alternatives, leave no space. The slash is also used in World Wide Web addresses.

pass/fail   and/or

He reiterated Milton's great lines: "The mind is its own place, and in itself / Can make a Heaven of Hell, a Hell of Heaven."

<http://www.whitehouse.gov>

23f   Parentheses

Use parentheses to enclose supplementary or less important material added as further explanation or example or to enclose figures or letters that enumerate a list.

The newest officers of the club (those elected in May) were installed at the ceremony.

They had three items on the agenda: (1) a revised budget, (2) the parking permits, and (3) a new election procedure.

23g   Brackets

Use brackets to add your comments or additional explanation within a quotation and to replace parentheses within parentheses. The Latin word *sic* in brackets means that you copied the original quotation exactly as it appeared, but you think there's an error there.

We all agreed with Fellner's claim that "this great team [the Chicago Bears] is destined to go to the Super Bowl next year."

The lawyer explained, "We discussed the matter in a fiendly [*sic*] manner."

For the use of brackets around ellipsis points in MLA format, see 23h.

23h   Omitted words/ellipsis

Use an ellipsis (a series of three periods, with one space between each period) to indicate that you are omitting words or part of a sentence from the source you are quoting. If you omit a whole sentence or paragraph, add a fourth period with no space after the last word preceding the ellipsis.

"modern methods . . . with no damage."

"the National Forest System . . . " (Smith 9).

"federal lands. . . . They were designated for preservation."

If you omit words immediately after a punctuation mark in the original, include that mark in your sentence.

"because of this use of the forest, . . . "

V
Mechanics

Contents of this section

QUESTION & CORRECT

The sections in this part of the book contain the rules for
matters of mechanics, including capitalization, italics,
numbers, abbreviations, and spelling.

                        SECTION   **PAGE**

24

Capitalization

24a Proper nouns vs. common nouns

Capitalize proper nouns, words that name one particular thing, most often a person or place rather than a general type or group of things.

Listed here are categories of words that should be capitalized. If you are not sure about a particular word, check your dictionary.

Proper noun	Common noun
James Joyce	man
Thanksgiving	holiday
University of Maine	state university
Macintosh	personal computer
May	spring

---

hint

Capitalizing Academic Subjects

Remember that general names of academic subjects, such as "history" or "economics," are not capitalized. However, the name of a specific department will be capitalized: the History Department. (This proper noun describes a particular department. Another history department might be called the Department of Historical Studies.)

- *Persons*

  Caitlin Baglia　　Hannah Kaplan　　Masuto Tatami

- *Places, including geographical regions*

  Indianapolis　　Ontario　　Midwest

- *Peoples and their languages*

  Spanish　　Dutch　　English

- *Religions and their followers*

  Buddhist   Judaism   Christianity

- *Members of national, political, racial, social, civic, and athletic groups*

  Democrat   African American   Chicago Bears
  Friends of   Danes   Olympics
    the Library   Committee

- *Institutions and organizations*

  Supreme Court   Legal Aid Society   Lions Club

- *Historical documents*

  Magna Carta   Declaration of Independence

- *Periods and events (but not century numbers)*

  Middle Ages   Boston Tea Party   eighteenth century

- *Days, months, and holidays (but not seasons)*

  Monday   Thanksgiving   winter

- *Trademarks*

  Coca-Cola   Kodak   Ford

- *Holy books and words denoting the Supreme Being (including pronouns)*

  Talmud   wonders of His creation   the Bible

- *Words and abbreviations derived from specific names (but not the names of things that have lost the specific association and now refer to the general type)*

  Stalinism   NATO   CBS
  french fry   pasteurize   italics

- *Place words ("City" or "Mountain") that are part of specific names*

  New York City   Zion National Park   Wall Street

- *Titles that precede people's names (but not titles that follow names)*

  Aunt Sylvia   President Taft   Governor Sam Parma
  Sylvia, my aunt   Sam Parma, governor

- *Words that indicate family relationships when used as a substitute for a specific name*

  Here is a gift for Mother. She sent a gift to her mother.

- *Titles of books, magazines, essays, movies, and other works, but not articles ("a," "an," "the"), short prepositions ("to," "by," "on"), or short joining words ("and," "or") unless they are the first or last word. With hyphenated words, capitalize the first and other important words. (For APA style, which has different rules, see section 41.)*

  The Taming of the Shrew   "The Sino-Soviet Conflict"

  A Dialogue Between Body   "My Brother-in-Law"
  and Soul

- *The pronoun "I" and the interjection "O" (but not the word "oh")*

  "Sail on, sail on, O ship of state," I said as the canoe sank.

- *Words placed after a prefix that are normally capitalized*

  un-American   anti-Semitic   ex-wife

24b   Capitals in sentences, quotations, and lists

- Capitalize the first word in a sentence.

- Capitalize the first word of a sentence in parentheses but not when the parenthetical sentence is inserted within another sentence.

- Do not capitalize the first word in a series of questions in which the questions are not full sentences.

  What did the settlers want from the natives? food? horses?

- Capitalize the first word of directly quoted speech, but not for the second portion of interrupted direct quotations or quoted phrases or clauses integrated into the sentence.

  She answered, "No one will understand."

  "No one," she answered, "will understand."

  When Hemmings declined the nomination, he said that "this is not a gesture of support for the other candidate."

- The first word in a list after a colon if each item in the list is a complete sentence.

  The rule books were very clear: (1) No player could continue to play after committing two fouls. (2) Substitute players would be permitted only with the consent of the other team. (3) Every eligible player had to be designated before the game.

(or)

The rule books were very clear:

1. No player could continue to play after committing two fouls.
2. Substitute players would be permitted only with the consent of the other team.
3. Every eligible player had to be designated before the game.

25

Italics

When you are typing or writing by hand, use underlining (a printer's mark to indicate words to be set in italic type font) for the kinds of titles and names indicated in this section. If your computer has an italic font, use that instead of underlining.

italics type font = *italics*
underlining = <u>underlining</u>

25a Titles

Use italics for titles and names of long or complete works, including the following:

Books:	*Catcher in the Rye*
Magazines:	*Time*
Newspapers:	*The New York Times*
Works of art (visual and performance):	*Swan Lake*
Pamphlets:	*Coping with Diabetes*
Television and radio series (not titles of individual episodes):	*ER*
Films and videos:	*Star Wars: Revenge of the Sith*
Long plays:	*Macbeth*
Long musical works:	*Symphony in B Minor*
Long poems:	*Paradise Lost*
Software:	*PageMaker*
Recordings:	*Yellow Submarine*

- Do not italicize or use quotation marks for the Bible and other major religious works or for legal documents.

  Bible   Torah   Koran   the Constitution

- For shorter works or parts of whole works, use quotation marks (see section 22b).

25b Other uses of italics/underlining

- Names of ships, airplanes, and trains

  Queen Mary   *Boeing 757*   *Orient Express*

- Foreign words and scientific names of plants and animals

  in vino veritas   *Canis lupis*

- Words used as words or letters, numbers, and symbols used as examples or terms

  Some words, such as *Kleenex*, are brand names.
  The letters *ph* and *f* often have the same sound.

- Words being emphasized

  It *never* snows here in April.

  (Use italics or underlining for emphasis only sparingly.)

  Do not use italics or underlining for the following:

- Words of foreign origin that are now part of English:

  alumni   karate   hacienda

- Titles of your own papers

26

Numbers

Style manuals for different fields and companies vary. The suggestions for writing numbers offered here are generally useful as a guide for academic writing.

- Spell out numbers that can be expressed in one or two words and use figures for other numbers.

Words	**Figures**
two pounds	126 days
six million dollars	$31.95
thirty-one years	6.381 bushels
eighty-three people	4.6 liters

- When you write several numbers, be consistent in choosing words or figures.

He didn't know whether to buy ~~nine~~ 9 gallons of milk or 125 separate small containers.

1. Use figures for the following:

    - **Days and years**
      December 12, 2005   (or)   12 December 2005
      A.D. 1066
      in 1998–99   (or)   in 1998–1999
      the 1990's   (or)   the 1990s

    - **Time of day**
      8 p.m. (or) P.M.   (or)   eight o'clock in the evening
      2:30 a.m. (or) A.M.   (or)   half past two in the morning

    - **Addresses**
      15 Tenth Avenue
      350 West 114 Street   (or)   350 West 114th Street
      Prescott, AZ 86301

    - **Identification numbers**
      room 8   channel 18
      Interstate 65   Henry VIII

    - **Page and division of books and plays (some instructors prefer roman numerals for volumes, parts, books, and chapters)**
      page 30   chapter 6
      bk. 5, ch. 7   *Hamlet* 2.9.7–10

    - **Decimals and percentages**
      2.7 average   12 and 1/2 percent
      0.036 metric ton

- **Numbers in series and statistics**
  two apples, six oranges, and three bananas
  115 feet by 90 feet

  (Be consistent whichever form you choose.)

- **Large round numbers**

  | four billion dollars | (or) | $4 billion |
  | 16,500,000 | (or) | 16.5 million |

- **Repeated numbers (in legal or commercial writing)**
  The bill will not exceed one hundred (100) dollars.

2. Do not use figures for the following:

- **Numbers that can be expressed in one or two words**
  the eighties   the twentieth century

- **Dates when the year is omitted**
  June sixth   May fourteenth

- **Numbers beginning a sentence**
  Ten percent of the year's crop was harvested.

27

Abbreviations

In government, business, and the fields of social science, science, and engineering, abbreviations are used frequently. But in academic writing in the humanities, only a limited number of abbreviations are generally used.

27a Abbreviating titles

- *Mr., Mrs.*, and *Ms.* are abbreviated when used as titles before the name.

  Mr. Tanato   Mrs. Whitman   Ms. Begay

- Dr. and St. ("Saint") are abbreviated only when they immediately precede a name; they are written out when they appear after the name.

  Dr. Martin Klein   (but)   Martin Klein, doctor of
                                                          pediatrics

- *Prof., Sen., Gen., Capt.*, and similar abbreviated titles can be used when they appear in front of a name or before initials and a last name. But they are not abbreviated when they appear with the last name only.

  Gen. R. G. Fuller   (but)   General Fuller

- *Sr., Jr., Ph.D., M.F.A., C.P.A.*, and other abbreviated academic titles and professional degrees can be used after the name.

  Lisle Millen, Ph.D.   Charleen Dyer, C.P.A.

- *Bros., Co.*, and similar abbreviations are used only if they are part of the exact name.

  Marshall Field & Co.   Brown Bros.

27b Abbreviating places

In general, spell out names of states, countries, continents, streets, rivers, and so on. But there are several exceptions:

- Use the abbreviation *D.C.* in Washington, D.C.

- Use *U.S.* only as an adjective, not as a noun.

  U.S. training bases   training bases in the United States

- If you include a full address in a sentence, citing the street, city, and state, you can use the postal abbreviation for the state.

  For further information, write to the company at 100 Peachtree Street, Atlanta, GA 30300 for a copy of their catalog.

  (but)

  The company's headquarters in Atlanta, Georgia, will soon be moved.

27c   Abbreviating numbers

- Write out numbers that can be expressed in one or two words.

  nine   twenty-seven   135

- The dollar sign abbreviation is generally acceptable when the whole phrase will be more than three words.

  $36 million   one million dollars

- For temperatures, use words if only a few temperatures are cited, but use figures if temperatures are cited frequently in a paper.

  ten degrees below zero, Fahrenheit   −10° F

27d   Abbreviating measurements

Spell out units of measurement, such as acre, meter, foot, and percent, but use abbreviations in tables, graphs, and figures.

27e   Abbreviating dates

Spell out months and days of the week. With dates and times, the following are acceptable:

57 A.D.   (or)   B.C.E. (Before the Common Era)
A.D. 329 (The abbreviation *A.D.* is placed before the date.)
a.m., p.m.   (or)   A.M., P.M.
EST   (or)   E.S.T., est

27f   Abbreviating names of familiar organizations and other entities

Use abbreviations for names of organizations, agencies, countries, and things usually referred to by their capitalized initials.

NASA	IBM	VCR	AFL-CIO
UNICEF	USSR	CNN	YMCA

If an abbreviation may not be familiar to your readers, spell out the term the first time you use it, with the abbreviation in parentheses. From then on, you can use the abbreviation.

The Myer-Briggs Type Inventory (MBTI) is offered in the dean's Career Counseling Office. Students who take the MBTI can then speak to a career counselor about the results.

27g   Abbreviating Latin expressions and documentation terms

Some Latin expressions always appear as abbreviations:

Abbreviation	Meaning
cf.	compare
e.g.	for example
et al.	and others
etc.	and so forth
vs. (or) v.	versus
N.B.	note well

These abbreviations are appropriate for bibliographies and footnotes, as well as in informal writing, but for formal writing, use the English phrase instead.

Because the format for abbreviations in documentation may vary from one style manual to another, use the abbreviations listed in the particular style manual you are following. (See, for example, the suggestions for MLA and APA in sections 40–41.)

Abbreviation	Meaning
abr.	abridged
anon.	anonymous
ed., eds.	editor, editors
p., pp.	page, pages
vol., vols.	volume, volumes

28

Spelling

English spelling is difficult because it contains so many words from other languages that have different spelling conventions. In addition, unlike some other languages that have only one spelling for a sound, English has several ways to spell some sounds. But it's important to spell correctly, to be sure that your reader understands your writing. Also, misspelled words can signal to the reader that the writer is careless and not very knowledgeable.

Because no writer wants to lose credibility, correct spelling is necessary. These suggestions should help to ensure that your papers are spelled correctly:

- **Learn some spelling rules.**

  See the following pages for some useful rules.

- **Learn your own misspelling patterns and troublesome words.**

  When you identify a word that tends to cause you problems, write it down in a list and, if possible, make up your own memory aid. For example, if you can't remember whether "dessert" is that barren sandy place like the Mohave (or Sahara) or the sweet treat you eat after a meal, try making up some rule or statement that will stick in your mind. For "dessert" and "desert," you might try a reminder such as the fact that the word for the sweet treat has two s's, and you like seconds on desserts.

- **Use a spell checker.**

  Spell checkers are helpful tools, but they can't catch all spelling errors. Although different spell checking programs have different capabilities, they are not foolproof, and they do make mistakes. Most spell checkers do not catch the following types of errors:

  1. **Omitted words**
  2. **Sound-alike words (homonyms)**
     Some words sound alike but are spelled differently. For example, the spell checker cannot distinguish between "there" and "their."
  3. **Substitution of one word for another**
     If you meant to write "one" and typed "own" instead, the spell checker will not flag that.
  4. **Proper nouns**
     Some well-known proper nouns, such as "Washington," may be in the spell checker, but many will not be.

5. **Misspelled words**
   If you have misspelled a word, the spell checker may be able to suggest the correct spelling. But for other misspellings, the spell checker will not be able to offer the correct spelling. You will need to know how to use a dictionary to look it up.

- **Learn how to proofread.**

  Proofreading requires slow and careful reading to catch misspellings and typographical errors. This is hard to do because we are used to reading quickly and seeing a group of words together. Some useful proofreading strategies are the following:

  1. **Slow down.**
     For best results, slow down your reading rate so you actually see each word.
  2. **Focus on each word.**
     One way to slow down is to point a pencil or pen at each word as you say it aloud or to yourself. Note with a check in the margin any word that doesn't look quite right, and come back to it later.
  3. **Read backward.**
     Don't read right to left, as you usually do, or you will soon slip back into a more rapid reading rate. Instead, move backward through each line from right to left. In this way, you won't be listening for meaning or checking for grammatical errors.
  4. **Cover up distractions.**
     To focus on each word, hold a sheet of paper or a notecard under the line being read. That way you won't be distracted by other words on the page.

28a Some spelling guidelines

1. **ie/ei**

> Write *i* before *e*
> Except after *c*
> Or when sounded like "ay"
> As in "neighbor" or "weigh."

This rhyme reminds you to write *ie*, except under two conditions:

- When the two letters follow a *c*
- When the two letters sound like "ay" (as in "day")

Some *ie* words		**Some *ei* words**	
believe	niece	ceiling	eight
chief	relief	receive	conceit
field	yield	vein	deceive

Some exceptions to this rule

conscience	foreign	neither	species
counterfeit	height	science	sufficient
either	leisure	seize	weird

2. **Doubling consonants**

   - **One-syllable words**

     If the word ends in a single short vowel and then a consonant, double the last consonant when you add a suffix beginning with a vowel.

drag	dragged	dragging
star	starred	starring
tap	tapped	tapping
wet	wetted	wetting

   - **Two-syllable words**

     If the word has two or more syllables and then a single vowel and a consonant, double the consonant when (1) you are adding a suffix that begins with a vowel, and (2) the last syllable of the base word is accented.

begin		beginning
occur	occurred	occurring
omit	omitted	omitting
prefer	preferred	preferring
refer	referred	referring

3. **Final silent –e**

   Drop the final silent –e when you add a suffix beginning with a vowel. But keep the final –e when the suffix begins with a consonant.

line	lining	care	careful
smile	smiling	like	likely

   Words such as "true/truly" and "argue/argument" are exceptions to this.

4. **Plurals**

Generally, most words add –*s* for plurals. But add –*es* when the word ends in –*s*, –*sh*, –*ch*, –*x*, or –*z* because another syllable is needed.

one apple	two apples
one box	two boxes
a brush	some brushes

With phrases and hyphenated words, pluralize the last word unless another word is more important.

one videocassette recorder	two videocassette recorders
one sister-in-law	two sisters-in-law

For words ending in a consonant plus –*y*, change the –*y* to –*i* and add –*es*. For proper nouns, keep the –*y*.

one boy	two boys
one company	two companies
Mr. Henry	the Henrys

For some words, the plural is formed by changing the base word. Some other words have the same form for singular and plural. And other words, taken from other languages, form the plural in the same way as the original language.

one child	two children
one woman	two women
one deer	two deer
one datum	much data
one medium	many media
a phenomenon	some phenomena

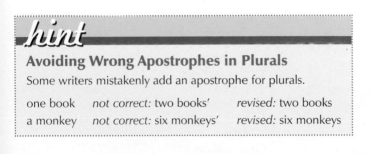

hint

Avoiding Wrong Apostrophes in Plurals
Some writers mistakenly add an apostrophe for plurals.

one book	*not correct:* two books'	*revised:* two books
a monkey	*not correct:* six monkeys'	*revised:* six monkeys

28b   Sound-alike words (homonyms)

Word	Meaning	Example
accept:	to agree/receive	accept a gift
except:	other than	all except her
affect:	to influence	Insomnia affects me.
effect:	a result	What was the effect?
hear:	(verb)	Did you hear that?
here:	indicates a place	Come here.
its:	shows possession	Its leg is broken.
it's:	= it is	It's raining out.
quiet:	no noise	Be quiet!
quite:	very	That's quite nice.
quit:	give up	He quit his job.
than:	used to compare	taller than I
then:	time word	Then he went home.
to:	preposition	to the house
too:	also (or) very	She is too tired to work.
were:	(verb)	were singing
we're:	= we are	We're going on vacation.
where:	in what place	Where is he?
who's:	= who is	Who's going to the movies?
whose:	shows possession	Whose book is this?
your:	shows possession	What is your name?
you're:	= you are	You're right!

VI
Multilingual Speakers (ESL)

Contents of this section

QUESTION & CORRECT

The sections in this part include topics that are especially useful for students whose first language is not English.

29

American Style in Writing/ESL Resources

American style

If your first language is not English, you may have some writing style preferences and some questions about English grammar and usage. Some of these matters will be addressed in this section. If you have individual questions and are a student at an institution with a writing center, talk with a tutor in the writing center.

Your style preferences and customs will depend on what language(s) you are more familiar with, but in general, consider the following differences between the language(s) you know and academic style in American English. Academic style in American English is characterized by the following:

Conciseness

In some languages, writers strive for a type of eloquence marked by a profusion of words and phrases that elaborate on the same topic. Effective academic and public writing in American English, however, is concise, eliminating extra or unnecessary words.

Clearly announced topic at the beginning of the paper

In some languages, the topic is delayed or not immediately announced. Instead, there are suggestions that will lead readers to formulate the main ideas for themselves. In American English, there is a decided preference for announcing the topic in the opening paragraph or somewhere near the beginning of the paper.

Tight organization

Although digressions into side topics or related matters can be interesting and are expected in the writing in some languages, American academic writing stays on topic and does not wander off into other topics.

Clearly cited sources

In some languages, there is less attention to citing sources of information, ideas, or the exact words used by others. In American academic writing, however, writers are expected to cite all sources other than what is generally known by most people. Otherwise, the writer is in danger of being viewed as plagiarizing. (See 38e.)

When you are considering matters of grammar and usage, sections 30 to 35 cover topics that may cause difficulty as you write in English. When you want other resources to learn English, see section 29b.

29b Resources for learning English as a second language

Some Web sites where you can find useful resources for learning English as another language include the following:

<http://dictionary.cambridge.org>
  Cambridge Dictionaries Online has several dictionaries to consult, including dictionaries for learners, for American English, for idioms (see section 35), and for two-word (phrasal) verbs (see section 30c). There are also links to online activities and worksheets.
<http://esl.fis.edu>
  Frankfort International School "Guide to Learning English"
<http://www.1-language.com>
  1-Language.com's site has links to services, chat rooms, etc.
<http://www.eslcafe.com>
  Dave Sperling's ESL Café includes a help center, materials, chat room, etc.
<http://www.eltweb.com/liason>
  ELT Web includes an index of English language resources
<http://www.eslgold.com/site.jsp?resource>
  ESL Gold has materials on writing, grammar, speaking, reading, vocabulary, etc.
<http://owl.english.purdue.edu/handouts/esl/eslstudent.html>
  Purdue University's OWL ESL resources for students has an extensive list of links to Web sites for ESL students
<http://www.rong-chang.com>
  English as a second language: an extensive site with a variety of materials

30

Verbs

Unlike some other languages, verbs are required in English sentences because they indicate time and person (see section 13b).

30a Verb tenses

Progressive tenses: use a form of "be" plus –*ing* form of the verb such as "going" or "running."

She <u>is</u> going to the concert tonight.

The plane's propellers <u>are spinning</u>.

Perfect tenses: use a form of "have" plus the past participle, such as "walked" or "gone."

No one <u>has talked</u> to me about that.

They <u>have gone</u> to the football game.

1. **Present tense**
    - Simple present
    presents action or condition
        They <u>ride</u> their bikes.
        He <u>seems</u> unhappy.
    general or literary truth
        States <u>defend</u> their rights.
        Shakespeare <u>uses</u> humor effectively.
    habitual action
        I <u>like</u> orange juice for breakfast.
        Her cell phone <u>rings</u> too loudly.
    future time
        The plane <u>arrives</u> at 10 p.m. tonight.
    - Present progressive
    activity in progress, not finished, or continued
        I <u>am majoring</u> in engineering.
        They <u>are living</u> in Mexico.

- Present perfect

  action that began in the past and leads up to and continues into the present

  He <u>has worked</u> here since May.

  I <u>have</u> not <u>seen</u> her in several days.

- Present perfect progressive

  action begun in the past, continues to the present, and may continue into the future

  I <u>have been thinking</u> about buying a car.

  They <u>have been planning</u> their trip to India for more than a year.

2. **Past tense**

- Simple past

  completed action or condition

  She <u>walked</u> to class.

  He <u>drove</u> to work.

- Past progressive

  past action over a period of time or interrupted by another action

  The engine <u>was running</u> while he waited.

  Everyone <u>was looking</u> the other way when she entered the room.

- Past perfect

  action or event completed before another event in the past

  He <u>had</u> already <u>left</u> when I arrived.

  The movie <u>had</u> already <u>started</u> when he took his seat.

- Past perfect progressive

  ongoing condition in the past that has ended

  She <u>had been speaking</u> to that group.

  Who <u>had been watching</u> the heating coil when it burned out?

3. **Future tense**

- Simple

  actions or events in the future

  > They <u>will arrive</u> tomorrow.

  > I <u>will return</u> the book next week.

- Future progressive

  future action that will continue for some time

  > I <u>will be expecting</u> you.

  > No one <u>will be using</u> that computer tomorrow.

- Future perfect

  actions that will be completed by or before a specified time in the future

  > By Monday, I <u>will have cleaned up</u> that cabinet.

  > The report <u>will have been finished</u> by the time the discussion starts.

- Future perfect progressive

  ongoing actions or conditions until a specified time in the future

  > She <u>will have been traveling</u> for six months by the time she arrives here.

  > By next Thursday, I <u>will have been visiting</u> my parents for three weeks.

30b   Helping verbs with main verbs

Helping (or auxiliary) verbs combine with other verbs. (See section 13b.)

be:	"be," "am," "is," "are," "was," "were," "being," "been"
do:	"do," "does," "did"
have:	"have," "has," "had"
modals:	"can," "could," "may," "might," "must," "shall," "should," "will," "would," "ought to"

Modal verbs are helping verbs that indicate possibility, uncertainty, necessity, or advisability. Use the base form of the verb after a modal.

> <u>May</u> I <u>ask</u> you a question?
> <u>Will</u> you <u>need</u> someone to meet you when your plane lands?
> <u>Can</u> someone <u>open</u> this large container?
> I <u>would like</u> some coffee, please.

30c Two-word (phrasal) verbs

Some verbs are followed by a second (and sometimes a third) word that combine to indicate the meaning. Many dictionaries will indicate the meanings of these phrasal verbs.

look over (examine):	She <u>looked over</u> the contract.
look up (search):	I will <u>look up</u> his phone number.
look out for (watch for):	<u>Look out for</u> the puddle.

The second word of some of these verbs can be separated from the main verb by a noun or pronoun:

> add (it) up   put (the phone call) off

In other cases, the second word cannot be separated from the main verb:

> back out of the garage   get through the mob

30d Verbs with –*ing* and with "to" + verb form

Some verbs combine only with the –*ing* form of the verb; some verbs combine only with the "to" + verb form (the infinitive form); some verbs can be followed by either form.

Verbs followed only by –*ing* forms:

admit	enjoy	recall
appreciate	finish	regret
deny	keep	risk
dislike	practice	suggest

He <u>admits spending</u> that money.

I <u>enjoy listening</u> to music.

Verbs followed only by "to" + verb:

agree	have	plan
ask	mean	promise
claim	need	wait
decide	offer	want

She <u>needs to take</u> that medicine.

They <u>asked to come</u> along with us.

Verbs that can be followed by either form:

begin	like	remember
continue	love	start
hate	prefer	try

They <u>begin to sing</u>. (or) They <u>begin singing</u>.

I <u>love to work</u> in my garden. (or) I <u>love working</u> in my garden.

31

Nouns (Count and Noncount)

There are two kinds of nouns—proper nouns and common nouns. Proper nouns name specific things (such as Lake Michigan or Mexico) and begin with capital letters (see section 24). Other nouns are common nouns, and they are either nouns that can be counted (count nouns) or nouns that cannot be counted (noncount nouns).

Count nouns: name things that can be counted because those things can be divided into separate and distinct units. Count nouns have plurals and usually refer to things that can be seen, heard, touched, tasted, or smelled.

apple:	one apple, some apples
chair:	a chair, six chairs
child:	the child, all of the children

Noncount nouns: name things that cannot be counted because they are abstractions or things that cannot be cut into parts. Noncount nouns do not have plurals, do not have "a" or "an" preceding them, and may have a collective meaning.

Some noncount nouns:

air	humor	oil	weather
furniture	money	beauty	clothing

To indicate amounts for noncount nouns, use a count noun that quantifies:

a pound of coffee	a loaf of bread
a quart of milk	a great deal of money

Noncount Nouns

Many foods are noncount nouns:

coffee	tea	corn	water
cereal	milk	candy	flour

32
Articles ("A," "An," and "The")

A/An

"A" and "an" identify nouns in a general or indefinite way and refer to any member of a group. "A" and "an" are generally used with singular count nouns.

Please hand me a towel.

(This sentence does not specify which towel, just any towel that is handy.)

The

"The" identifies a particular or specific noun in a group or a noun already specified in a previous phrase or sentence. "The" may be used with singular or plural nouns.

Please hand me <u>the</u> towel that is on the table.

(This sentence means that not just any towel is being requested—only the one particular towel that is on the table.)

<u>A</u> new computer model is being introduced. <u>The</u> new model will probably cost more.

("A" is used first in a general way to mention the model, and then, because it has been specified, it is referred to as "the" model.)

Some uses of "the"

- Use "the" when an essential phrase or clause follows the noun.

  <u>The</u> man who addressed the group is my art teacher.

- Use "the" when the noun refers to a class as a whole.

  He explained that <u>the</u> fox is a nocturnal animal.

- Use "the" with names composed partly of common nouns and plural nouns.

  <u>the</u> British Commonwealth   <u>the</u> United States
  <u>the</u> Netherlands   <u>the</u> University of Illinois

- Use "the" with names that refer to rivers, oceans, seas, deserts, forests, gulfs, and peninsulas and with points of the compass used as names.

  <u>the</u> Nile   <u>the</u> Persian Gulf   <u>the</u> South

- Use "the" with superlatives

  <u>the</u> best reporter   <u>the</u> most expensive car

No articles

Articles are not used with names of streets, cities, states, countries, continents, lakes, parks, mountains, names of languages, sports, holidays, universities, and academic subjects.

He traveled to Africa.   She is studying Chinese.
He likes to watch tennis.   He graduated from Brandeis.

33

Prepositions

Prepositions in English show relationships between words and are difficult to master because they are idiomatic. The following lists some of the most commonly used prepositions and the relationships they indicate. For prepositions not listed here and for other uses of the prepositions explained here, check a dictionary.

Prepositions of time

On	• used with days
	<u>on</u> Monday
At	• used with hours of the day
	<u>at</u> 9 a.m., <u>at</u> noon
In	• used with other parts of the day
	<u>in</u> the afternoon

Prepositions of place

On	• indicates a surface on which something rests
	The car was parked <u>on</u> the street.
At	• indicates a point in relation to another subject
	My sister is <u>at</u> home.
In	• indicates a subject is inside the boundaries of an area or volume
	The sample is <u>in</u> the bottle.
	She lives <u>in</u> Chicago.

Prepositions to show logical relationships

Of	• shows relationship between a part and the whole
	Two <u>of</u> her teachers gave quizzes today.

•shows material or content

That basket <u>of</u> fruit is a present.

For   •shows purpose

He bought some plants <u>for</u> the garden.

With   •shows a means used

He dug the hole <u>with</u> a shovel.

•shows cause or origin

He was sick <u>with</u> the flu.

•shows possession

The house <u>with</u> the porch belongs to me.

34

Omitted/Repeated Words

34a   Omitted words

Subjects and verbs can be omitted in some languages, but they are necessary in English sentences and must appear. The only exception in English is the command that has an understood subject: "Put that box here." (The understood subject here is "you.")

Subjects

Include a subject in the main clause and in all other clauses as well. "There" and "it" may sometimes serve as subject words.

All the children laughed while _{they} were watching cartoons.

_{It is} Is raining today.

Verbs

Although verbs such as "is" and "are" and helping verbs can be omitted in some languages, they must appear in English.

> *is*
> She ⌃ an effective Spanish teacher.

> *has*
> No one ⌃ gone to the lecture.

34b   Repeated words

In some languages, the subject can be repeated as a pronoun before the verb. However, in English, the subject is included only once.

> Bones in the body ~~they~~ become brittle as people grow older.

In some languages, objects of verbs or prepositional phrases are repeated, but not in English.

> The woman tried on the hat that I left ~~it~~ on the seat.
> The city where I live ~~there~~ has two soccer fields.

35

Idioms

An idiom is an expression that means something beyond the simple definition or literal translation into another language. An idiom such as "kick the bucket" (meaning "die") is not understandable from the meanings of the individual words.

Dictionaries of American English idioms can define many of the commonly used ones. The second word in two-word verb phrases (phrasals, see section 30b) is idiomatic and changes meanings.

> bottom line = the last figure on a financial sheet; the
> result or final outcome or ultimate truth

dark horse = someone not likely to be the winner
under the table = something done illegally
to turn <u>off</u> the light = to shut the light, to stop it
to set an alarm to go <u>off</u> = to make an alarm work, to
start it
to live <u>up</u> to = to put into practice, to meet some standard
to live <u>with</u> = to share a residence with, to tolerate

VII
Research

....

Contents of this section

QUESTION & CORRECT

The sections in this part cover the process of doing research in print and online sources, finding and narrowing a topic, using Web resources, evaluating and integrating information, and following document design principles. You'll also find discussions of summaries, paraphrases, and quotations, as well as plagiarism and how to avoid it.

36

Doing Print and Online Research

Some research papers that present your findings may be objective and discuss only the information you found but not your opinion or perspective on the topic. Other research papers may be persuasive because, after presenting the information you found, you come to conclusions or argue your opinion or viewpoint. Be sure that you know which is the appropriate goal as you write the paper.

Doing research is a process of selecting a topic, formulating the research question(s) you will address, searching for information, taking notes, keeping a list of the citations, evaluating what you have found, organizing the material, writing the paper, including adequate support for your thesis, and citing your sources.

36a Selecting a topic

There are four steps to selecting a topic:

1. **Find** a general subject that interests you (if one has not been assigned) and that fits your assignment, your goal, and your purpose (see section 1a).

   One way to locate an interesting subject is to think about a subject you'd like to know more about or one that has been a subject of controversy that you want to clarify in your own mind. Or you can browse through any book or catalog of subject headings such as the *Library of Congress Subject Headings* or the *Reader's Guide to Periodical Literature*. You can also consider the topics covered in a magazine you read or browse through journals in a field you are interested in to look at topics discussed there. (See section 36e for a resource list of journals you are likely to find in your library.) On the Web, you can browse through subject directories (see 36d for specific sites to try) or Web sites that you visit that interest you. Two examples of general subjects to start with are the following:

   Imagery in Maya Angelou's poetry

   Careers in technical writing

2. **Narrow** that subject to a topic to fit the assignment and the length of the paper that will be written. How much time will you have to do the research? How long will the paper be? To narrow a topic, start by thinking about how to make it more specific and manageable.

Too broad: A topic that is too broad will have too many subtopics to cover in any manageable way. Suppose you start with world hunger as a topic. Think of some subtopics that would have to be included. In the case of world hunger, some areas to cover would include causes, extent in terms of populations and geography, possible solutions, cost, political considerations, and so on. This is far too much to cover and is, therefore, too broad.

Too narrow: A topic that is too narrow has very little information available to research. For example, if you were to decide to research the topic of the cost of producing racing bicycle tires, there really isn't much to find out other than contacting some companies that manufacture them. Or you might start with a topic such as whether hybrid cars are selling better than SUVs. That can be easily learned by getting the sales figures of both types of automobiles.

Too well known: There are topics that are no longer interesting because we know the answers or because the topic has been dealt with so often in the news that most people are no longer interested in it. For example, the topic of whether cigarette smoking is harmful to our health is already generally known and no longer controversial.

To make those general topics of Maya Angelou's poetry or careers in technical writing more specific, choose one possible subtopic such as the following:

Maya Angelou's use of fire imagery

Technical writing jobs in the computer industry

3. **Formulate a research question** about your topic. Your research question will help you decide what information is relevant. Try formulating the question with any of the reporter's "who," "what," "where," "why," "when," and "how" questions.

Why does Maya Angelou use fire imagery in her poetry?

What kinds of jobs are available in the computer industry for technical writing majors?

4. **Formulate a thesis statement** that answers your research question.

After completing your research and reviewing your information, you will be able to formulate a tentative thesis. This statement will answer your research question, but it may need to be revised somewhat as you write your paper.

> Maya Angelou uses images of fire in her poetry to convey cleansing and rebirth.

> In the computer industry, technical writing majors are hired to write documents such as computer manuals, training materials, and in-house newsletters.

36b Sources of information

The two categories of information to use are primary and secondary sources.

- **Primary sources**   Primary sources are original or firsthand materials such as the poem or novel by the author you are writing about. Other primary materials are surveys, speeches, interviews you conduct, or firsthand accounts of events. Primary sources are not filtered through a second person. They may be more accurate because they have not been distorted or misinterpreted by others.

- **Secondary sources**   Secondary sources are secondhand accounts, information, or reports about primary sources. Typical secondary sources include reviews, biographies about a person you are studying, documentaries, encyclopedia articles, news stories, and other materials interpreted, studied, or reported by others. Remember that secondary sources are interpretations or analyses that may be biased, inaccurate, or incomplete.

Library Sources

Your library is most useful for the following kinds of information:

- **Major works in the field (books, journals, references)**   Although many books, reference works, and other important resources are available on the Web, most major stud-

hint

ESL Stating Your Ideas

Although some cultures place more value on student writing that primarily brings together or collects the thoughts of great scholars or experts, readers of research papers in American institutions value the writer's own interpretations and thinking about the subject.

ies, histories, references, and other documents are in the library, not yet on the Internet. Some scholarly journals are available on the Web, and there are some electronic journals and magazines too, but they may require readers to subscribe or may make only a sampling of their contents available at no charge. Many major scholarly books and journals, reference works, and magazines are in your library, not on the Internet.

- **Historical sources and textbooks** Most older books and other materials such as textbooks that are important or useful sources of information will be in libraries, not on the Internet.

- **Databases** Your library is the place to look for those databases that charge or that require the purchase of a CD-ROM.

Libraries have various printed and online guides for users and an information desk where you can talk with helpful librarians. In addition to the print and online catalogs available through your library, you can access other libraries with online catalogs and databases (see 36d). Some useful indexes, catalogs, and databases that may be available through your library include the following:

- *Books in Print*

- *Reader's Guide to Periodical Literature*

- Encyclopedias such as *Collier's Encyclopedia* and more specialized ones such as the *Harvard Guide to American History* and the *Oxford Companion to English Literature*

- Abstracts and almanacs such as *Statistical Abstracts of the United States*

- Online searches of the library's holdings by author, title, key word, and subject heading

- *Library of Congress Subject Headings* (This is helpful for subject heading searches when working online and can suggest alternate ways of phrasing keywords for your topic.)

- The Library of Congress (It's the largest library in the world.)

- Electronic databases such as the following:
  Academic Search Elite
  Access Science
  American National Biography Online
  Business and Company Resource Center
  Business and Industry
  CINAHL: Cumulative Index to Nursing and Allied
      Health Literature
  ComAbstracts (Communications)
  Contemporary Authors
  Contemporary Literary Criticism Select
  Dictionary of Literary Biography
  EBSCOHost
  ERIC (Educational Resources Information Center)
  GPO Index (index of federal government publications)
  Humanities Abstracts
  LexisNexis
  Literary Resource Center
  MasterFILE Premier (wide range of subjects)
  MathSciNet
  MEDLINE
  NewsBank NewsFile (current issues in newspapers,
      wire services, and broadcasts)
  PsycINFO
  Social Sciences Abstracts
  Sport Discus

- Computerized bibliographic utilities such as *FirstSearch* (which accesses databases such as academic journals, corporations, congressional publications, and medical journals) or *Newsbank CD News* (which indexes articles from a variety of newspapers). Nexis/Lexis is a commercial service available online and has abstracts and full texts of magazines, newspapers, publications from industry and government, wire services, and other sources, but your library may have the Lexis/Nexis Academic database. Check your library's Web site.

Internet sources

Online searching for information can be very fruitful because it connects you to vast resources in distant places that you can access quickly and easily. But it's important to have a clear sense of which kinds of information are available online and which are better searched for in libraries or other sources such as the community or your campus. Specific Web sites to use when searching are listed in 36d.

The Internet is useful when searching for many types of information, and it is especially helpful when searching for the following:

- **Government sources**   The federal government has numerous sites on the Internet with large quantities of information produced by various government bureaus, departments, and agencies, in addition to information produced by legislative action. The Library of Congress is especially useful because of its huge collection of materials, the largest in the world. You can also check for references to appropriate government publications that your library may have on the shelves.

- **Library catalogs online**   You can search many libraries online to find other materials on your topic, materials that your library may not have and may be able to borrow for you. You can also read titles and abstracts to get a sense of what's available on the topic. These online catalogs are especially useful for compiling a working bibliography to start your search. Some of the major libraries online also have searchable databases and lists of resources in various areas that may be useful.

- **Current news**   The major American newspapers and magazines have Web sites where you can read about recent events or rapidly changing conditions, and you can search the sites for past information. In most cases, however, these archives go back only a few years, and some newspapers may charge a fee for these materials.

- **Nonprofit public interest groups**   Although there is a great deal of propaganda on the Internet put up by special-interest groups, some nonprofit organizations collect useful information on issues such as how to organize local citizen action groups, detect propaganda, identify Internet myths, fix various types of electronics, uncover media bias, and so on. However, other special-interest groups promote hate, fraudulent practices, violence, fear, and deception of various types. Be very careful when you enter the world of special-interest Web sites. The section on evaluating Internet sources, in 37c, will help you identify appropriate and unbiased sources. (Some special-interest sites, though, may help you identify arguments on various sides of an issue. For example, if you are researching an issue such as federal regulation of automobile emission standards, you'll find Web sites promoting a number of viewpoints. These will help you locate the arguments being made for and against various aspects of the issue.)

- **Some older books**   There are several projects, such as Project Bartleby, the English Server at Carnegie Mellon University, and Project Gutenberg, dedicated to making available online older books whose copyrights have expired. Other projects are dedicated to making rare or hard-to-find older resources available online. The search engine company Google is presently working on putting online digital versions of the books in some large libraries.

- **Information relevant to a field of study or major**   If you start with the sites listed in fields of study in 36e, you'll find the Web sites that have collected links to information about that field.

- **Images, photographs, art, and other online media**   There are hundreds of Web sites with photographs, including news media archives, museums, historical sites, and libraries (see 36d).

Community sources

Your community has a variety of resources to tap, including public records and other local government information in a city hall or county courthouse. Other sources are community service workers, social service agencies, school teachers and school administrators, community leaders, religious leaders, coordinators in nonprofit groups, the local chamber of commerce or visitors and convention bureau, local public library, museums or historical societies, the newspaper, and your campus offices and faculty.

Interviews and surveys

You can do field research by interviewing people, sending e-mail messages, conducting surveys, and taking notes on your own observations.

36c   Search engine strategies and options

1. Search Engine Strategies

- **Different types of tools available**

    - **Search engines**   Search engines work by search-ing among the contents of public sites on the Internet for key terms that you indicate. The search engine returns a list of sites that include the key term. Because various search engines work differently, each will turn up different results. Some results, however, may be promi-nently displayed because the site owner has paid to be listed at or near the top of the results list. (These are usually referred to as "sponsored links.") Be sure to read the search options the site offers so that you use it effectively. Also, some sites have their own search engines and site maps to help you find information on various parts of that site. And there are also metasearch engines, such as Dogpile.com, Metacrawler.com, and Momma.com that search other search engines and compile the results. For Web addresses of various search engines, see 36d.

    - **Subject categories or directories**   These indexes or directories organize Web resources by categories such as "health," "entertainment," and "business." Most have subdirectories under the main head-ings. These lists are particularly useful when you are looking for suggestions for a topic, for a quick look at the types of information available on that topic, or for ways to phrase key terms for searches. Yahoo.com is an example of a site with extensive lists of categories and subjects.

    - **Newsgroups and listservs**   Newsgroups are open forums on the Usenet network where anyone can post a message on the topic of the forum. Listservs are e-mail discussion groups in which participants have to subscribe to the list. Any message from any member of the listserv goes to all the subscribers. The listowner may or may not moderate what appears by controlling which messages get through to the list. On Google.com's homepage, you can select the "groups" option to search news-groups and listservs.

- **Blogs**   Blogs are Web logs that people write and post on the Web. There are thousands of blogs, containing the personal opinions of whoever puts them on the Web, and they are not likely to be reliable sources of information. There is no monitoring of the quality or reliability of blogs. But some blogs written by well-known specialists are read and quoted by many people. To help users to find people's blogs, various sites exist, such as globeofblogs.com, findory.com, or www.bestoftheblogs.com.
- **Web sites with collections of information**   In 36d and 36e, you will find addresses for many Web sites that compile large quantities of information. For example, the government sites listed in 36d will be collections of documents relevant to various areas of the government such as census data, congressional bills under consideration, world health surveys, and so on. In 36e you will find sites with many links to information in particular fields.

- **Different ways to search**
  Use your detective skills to think about different ways to start and which leads to follow. When you use some creative thinking, you'll find that you begin to think of a variety of kinds of sites, sites that are beyond the ordinary or expected ones.

  Sample search   Suppose your assignment is to research your major, and you want to learn more about job opportunities in that major. Here are some different ways to approach your search:

  - Go to general job search sites, such as Monster.com, to see what it has listed.
  - Try the resource lists and directories in that academic field (see 36d) because some of the Web sites listed will have relevant job opportunities listed.
  - Try university Web sites that have department pages and career centers that will include job opportunities.
  - Seek out sites that collect résumés or help companies find employees. (Some sites charge for these services.)
  - Look at U.S. Census report data to see what you can find there. In other federal government

sites, you'll find government studies of prospects for various fields.

- Try Web sites of large companies in that field to see what they list as job openings. (Some online yellow-pages search engines list the Web addresses in addition to the street and city locations.)
- Tune in to listservs and newsgroups of people in that area of work to see what they are discussing.
- Use a few search engines to see what they turn up. Some search engines include among their categories that of job seeking. (There will be some similarities in search engine listings, but there will also be different ones in each. But be prepared to find that the search engine turns up more items than you want to read.)

- **Ways to narrow searches**
  Keeping these suggestions in mind as you search will make your search more efficient:

  - To be more specific use phrases instead of single words as search terms. Be sure to enclose the phrase or term in quotation marks so that all the words appear together in the sites turned up by the search engine. For example, if you are looking for information about home construction, be sure to use quotation marks around the term ("home construction") so that the millions of sites with the word "home" (including all those with a link to the "home" page) aren't included.
  - Switch search terms if the one you are using doesn't turn up much that's useful.
  - Browse through the subject categories in a search engine such as Excite.com to see what terms relate to your subject.
  - Enclose the whole phrase or term in quotation marks to ensure that the entire term is the object of the search.
  - Start with a metasearch engine such as Dogpile.com, Mamma.com, or Metacrawler to search many search engines at once (see 36d).
  - When you find a useful site, look for links to other related sites.

- Use "and," "or," or "not" between terms.

   "AND" is used to join two terms that are related in your search. For example, use "John F. Kennedy" AND "assassination" when you are looking for information only about the assassination of this American president and not about the rest of his life.

   "OR" is useful when you have more than one option for terms related to your topic. For example, use "flu vaccines" OR "influenza vaccines" when you are searching for information about this.

   "NOT" is useful to eliminate unwanted sites that might relate to your search term. For example, use "identity theft" NOT "forgery" if you want to find information only about identity theft due to fraudulent use of credit cards and social security numbers.

2. **Search engine options**

   Search engines offer a variety of options when searching the Web. They differ in the ways they search, the categories of sites they search, the results that turn up, and the varieties of options for searching they offer. So, before using any search engine, read any explanations and choices offered on the site that will give you a better idea of how to use it effectively. You can find a list of search engine Web addresses in section 36d.

   As you will find out when you read what the search engine offers as options, you can limit your search by language, date, and so on. For example, AltaVista.com can translate short passages from one language to another; HotBot.lycos.com's advanced search option permits you to specify the date and language to search in, and on Google.com you can choose to search the entire Web, images only, or postings in newsgroups and listservs. Google.com and Yahoo.com offer options such as advanced searching too, which is explained on the site. And other search engines, such as Dogpile.com, are metasearch engines that search a collection of other search engines.

   When you view the results lists, you need to be aware of policies of the site. Google.com identifies sponsored links (links that companies pay for, to list prominently at the top of the list), but some other search engines may or may not indicate that the first few listings are there because some company paid to have you see them, not because they are the best match for what you are seeking.

36d   Web resources

The pages of Web resources listed here are categorized in the following way:

1. **Writing**
    Here you'll find links to style manuals; grammar and writing handouts; MLA, APA, and *Chicago Manual* sites; dictionaries; a thesaurus; *Bartlett's Familiar Quotations*; and information on business, social science, and technical writing.

    Use these sites for help with writing.

2. **General subjects**
    This is a particularly useful collection of links to huge subject directories; online books, journals, and newspapers; scholarly societies and electronic discussion groups; colleges; and search engines.

    Use these sites for initial searches across a broad area and for links to articles and books available online.

3. **Fields of study**
    In 36e you'll find links to sites that focus on specific fields of study such as education, history, science, engineering, and so on.

    Use these sites for more specialized information in a particular field of study. See also 36e for lists of journals and additional Web resources in various fields.

4. **Government**
    There are vast sites that link to all the government agencies and have online publications of data collected by all branches of the government, from health to population to governments of other countries.

    Use these sites for data, statistics, or studies you think might have been done by government agencies and for information about all branches of government and the work they do.

5. **Libraries online**
   These are links to online libraries. Many have search engines, databases that are available to all users, and collections of useful links.

   Use these links to find out what else has been written about your topic and what books and journals can be loaned to your library if it does not have those materials.

6. **Online media, images, art, photographs, and popular culture**
   These are links to online sources of visual elements.

   Use these links to add visual elements, such as pictures, photographs, and art to your documents.

1. **Writing**

   • **Writing guides**
     Strunk and White, *Elements of Style:* <http://www.bartleby.com/br/141.html>
     International Writing Centers Association OWLs: <http://www.writingcenters.org/owcdb/index.php>
     Purdue University: <http://owl.english.purdue.edu/handouts/index.html>
     Colorado State University: <http://writing.colostate.edu/>

   • **Writing in special fields**
     Business Writing: Purdue OWL: <http://owl.english.purdue.edu/handouts/pw/index.html>
     Engineering and Science Writing: <http://fbox.vt.edu/eng/mech/writing/>
     Social Science Writing: <http://www.emayzine.com/lectures/writing.htm>
     Scientific Writing: (See Engineering and Science Writing)

   • **References**
     Bartlett's Familiar Quotations: <http://www.bartleby.com/100/>
     Biographical Dictionary: <http://s9.com/biography>
     Encyclopedia Britannica: <http://www.britannica.com/>
     KnowPlay: <http://www.kplay.cc/reference.html>
     Merriam Webster Dictionary: <http://www.m-w.com/>

Online Dictionaries: <http://www.yourdictionary.
com/> <http://www.dictionary.com/>

Roget's Thesaurus: <http://www.bartleby.com/
thesauri>

2. **General subjects**

• **Search engines**

Many of these sites show sponsored links first, that
is, links to sites that have paid to have a prominent
listing. Google has sponsored links, but it indicates
that fact in its results list. It is also perhaps the most
comprehensive search engine.

Metasearch engines:
Dogpile: <http://www.dogpile.com>
Mamma.com: <http://www.mamma.com>
Metacrawler: <http://www.metacrawler.com>
Search engines:
AltaVista: <http://www.altavista.com>
Ask Jeeves: <http://ask.com>
Excite: <http://www.excite.com>
Google: <http://www.google.com>
Teoma: <http://www.teoma.com/>
Yahoo: <http://www.yahoo.com>

For a directory of search engines, see AllSearch
Engines.com, which briefly describes the largest
search engines on its home page, lists all search
engines on a separate page and offers a brief note
on each, and lists search engines for various
categories:
<http://www.allsearchengines.com/>

• **General subject directories**
Awesome Library: <http://www.awesomelibrary.
org/>
Internet Public Library: <http://www.ipl.org>
WWW Virtual Library: <http://vlib.org/>

• **Books online**
Electronic Text Center: <http://www-2.cs.cmu.edu/
afs/cs/user/phoebe/mosaic/stuff-to-read.html>
Online Books Page: <http://onlinebooks.library.
upenn.edu/>
Project Bartleby: <http://www.bartleby.com/>
Project Gutenberg: <http://promo.net/pg>

- **Electronic listservs and newsgroups**
  Tile.Net: <http://tile.net/lists/>
  Usenet: <http://www.faqs.org/faqs/>

- **Journals and periodicals online**
  Magazines, Journals, Periodicals Online <http://www.wam.umd.edu/~mlhall/magazines.html>

- **Newspapers, news services, e-zines, media, magazines online**
  ABC News: <http://abcnews.go.com/>
  CBS News: <http://www.cbsnews.com/>
  Chronicle of Higher Education: <http://chronicle.com>
  EcolaNewsstand: <http://www.ecola.com>
  E-Journal Site Guide: <http://www.library.ubc.ca/ejour/>
  FOX News: <http://www.foxnews.com/>
  Guardian Unlimited Online: <http://www.guardian.co.uk/>
  Google News: <http://news.google.com/>
  MSNBC: <http://www.msnbc.com/news/>
  National Public Radio: <http://www.npr.org>
  The New York Times: <http://nytimes.com>
  Reuters News Media: <http://www.reuters.com>
  The Wall Street Journal: <http://online.wsj.com/public/us>

- **Scholarly electronic conferences**
  ARL Office of Scholarly Communication: <http://www.arl.org/scomm/edir/>

- **Scholarly societies**
  Alliance for Computers and Writing: <http://www2.nau.edu/acw/>
  American Astronomical Society: <http://www.aas.org>
  American Institute of Physics: <http://www.aip.org>
  American Philosophical Society: <http://www.amphilsoc.org/>
  Association of Teachers of Technical Writing: <http://www.attw.org/>
  Council of Science Editors: <http://www.councilscienceeditors.org/>
  National Academy of Sciences: <http://www.nas.edu>
  National Council of Teachers of English: <http://www.ncte.org/>

Scholarly Societies Project: <http://www.scholarly-societies.org/>

- **Universities in the United States** <http://www.clas.ufl.edu/CLAS/american-universities.html>

3. **Fields of study**
   In 36e, pages 140–48, you'll find lists of magazines, journals, and Web sites that can be useful for searching for information in particular disciplines and fields of study.

4. **Government**

   - Bureau of the Census: <http://www.census.gov>
   - CIA: <http://www.odci.gov>
   - Fedworld: <http://www.fedworld.gov>
   - National Institutes of Health: <http://www.nih.gov>
   - Nonprofit Gateway: <http://www.nonprofit.gov>
   - Stat USA (business, trade, and economic information): <http://www. stat-usa.gov/>
   - Thomas: Legislative Information on the Internet: <http://thomas.loc.gov>
   - White House: <http://www.whitehouse.gov>
   - World Health Organization: <http://www.who.int/home-page/>

5. **Libraries online**

   - American Library Association: <http://www.ala.org>
   - Internet Public Library: <http://www.ipl.org>
   - Library of Congress: <http://lcweb.loc.gov>
   - Libweb: <http://sunsite.berkeley.edu/Libweb>
   - Time & Life Pictures: <http://www.timelifepictures.com/ms_timepix/source/home/home.aspx?pg=1>
   - Webseek: <http://persia.ee.columbia.edu:8008/>

6. **Online media, images, art, photographs, and popular culture**

   - About: Web clip art: <http://webclipart.about.com>
   - Advertising Museum: <http://www.halcyon.com/donace/MUSEUM.HTM>
   - Artcyclopedia: <http://www.artcyclopedia.com>
   - ImageFinder: <http://sunsite3.berkeley.edu/ImageFinder/>
   - *Images: A Journal of Film and Popular Culture:* <http://www.imagesjournal.com/>
   - Library of Congress: American Memory: <http://lcweb2.loc.gov/ammem/browse/>

36e   Sources in various disciplines

When you are seeking information in various fields of study, the following lists of magazines, journals, and Web sites should help you. Most of the magazines and journals listed here have Web sites, but many of them require users to be subscribers in order to read any of the contents online. Also, check the Web sites listed in 36d for additional resources also available online. In addition, an excellent place to search for particular fields is the Academic Information Index. It has a rich collection of links for most major academic fields of study: <http://www.academicinfo.net/table.html>.

American Studies: <http://www.georgetown.edu/crossroads/asainfo.html>

Art: Magazines and journals:

- *American Artist*
- *Artforum*
- *Art History*
- *Metropolis*

Art Museums:

- Art Institute of Chicago: <http://www.artic.edu>
- Louvre, France: <http://www.louvre.fr/>
- Metropolitan Museum, New York: <http://www.metmuseum.org>
- National Gallery, Washington, D.C.: <http://www.nga.gov/>

Web site:

- Art and Art History: <http://art-design.umich.edu/mother/>

Black History: Web sites:

- Black History Quest: <http://blackquest.com/link.htm>
- Black History: <http://www.britannica.com/Blackhistory/home.do;jsessionid=340A4BA5765893140038E3786190C4E0>

Biology: <u>Magazines and journals:</u>

- *JAMA: Journal of the American Medical Association*
- *Quarterly Review of Biology*

<u>Web sites:</u>

- Biology Online: <http://www.biology-online.org/>
- University of Arizona Biology Project: <http://www.biology.arizona.edu/>

Business/Economics/Management: <u>Magazines and journals:</u>

- *BusinessWeek*
- *Economist*
- *Harvard Business Review*
- *Journal of Business*
- *Sloan Management Review*

<u>Web sites:</u>

- Business.com (products, services, jobs, companies): <http://www.business.com/>
- CommerceNet: <http://www.commerce.net>
- CNN Money: <http://money.cnn.com/>

Chemistry: <u>Web sites:</u>

- Chemdex: <http://www.chemdex.org/>
- Chemistry.Org: <http://www.acs.org/portal/Chemistry>

Communication: <u>Journals:</u>

- *American Communication Journal:* <http://www.acjournal.org/>
- *Columbia Journalism Review:* <http://www.cjr.org>
- *Quarterly Journal of Speech*

<u>Web sites:</u>

- American Communication Association Online: <http://www.americancomm.org/>

- Concordia Libraries: Communications-Related Web Sites: <http://library.concordia.ca/research/subjects/communicationst/internet.php>
- National Communication Association: <http://www.natcom.org/nca/Template2.asp>

Composition and Rhetoric: <u>Journals:</u>

- *College Composition and Communication*
- *College English*

Computer Science: <u>Journals:</u>

- *Artificial Intelligence*
- *Byte*
- *Harvard Computer Review*
- *Technical Computing*

<u>Web sites:</u>

- State University of New York at Albany Computer Resources: <http://library.albany.edu/subject/csci.htm>
- Yahoo Computer Science directory: <http://dir.yahoo.com/Science/Computer_Science/>

Culture: <u>Journals:</u>

- *Common Knowledge*
- *Language, Society, and Culture*

Education: <u>Journals:</u>

- *Education Research and Perspectives*
- *Education Week*

<u>Web sites:</u>

- Educator's Reference Desk: <http://www.eduref.org/>
- Educational Technology: <http://www.educause.edu/>>
- ERIC database: <http://www.eric.ed.gov/>
- The Gateway to Educational Materials: <http://www.thegateway.org/>

Engineering: <u>Journals:</u>

- *Space Technology*
- *Automotive Engineering*
- *Industrial Engineering*

<u>Web site:</u>

- Engineering Association and Directory:
  <http://www.engineers-international.com/
  instituteindex.html>

English as a second language: <u>Web sites:</u>

- Dave's English Language Café:
  <http://www.eslcafe.com/>
- English as 2nd Language:
  <http://esl.about.com/>
- English as a Second Language:
  <http://www.rong-chang.com/>
- ESL/EFL Resources Online: <http://www.
  arts.mcgill.ca/programs/esl/csamuel/#4>

Environmental Studies: <u>Magazines and journals:</u>

- *Amicus*
- *Atmospheric Environment*
- *Center for Health and the Global
  Environment Newsletter*
- *The Earth Times*
- *Environmental Health Perspectives Journals*

<u>Web sites:</u>

- About Environmental Issues:
  <http://environment.about.com/>
- Best Environmental Resources Directory:
  <http://www.ulb.ac.be/ceese/meta/cds.
  html>
- EnviroInfo: <http://www.deb.uminho.pt/
  fontes/enviroinfo/>
- Environmental Issues: <http://www.
  globalissues.org/EnvIssues/>
- Greenpeace:
  <http://www.greenpeace.org.uk/>

- National Council for Science and the Environment: <http://www.ncseonline.org/NLE/CRS/>
- Sierra Club: <http:// www.sierraclub.org>

Foreign Language and Literature: <u>Web sites:</u>

- Academic Info Foreign Lang Study: <http://www.academicinfo.net/lang.html>
- Foreign Language Resources on the WWW: <http://www.cortland.edu/flteach/flteach-res.html>

History: <u>Magazines and journals:</u>

- *American Historical Review*
- *American History*
- *English Literary History*
- *History Today*
- *Journal of Social History*
- *Journal of Modern History*
- *Journal of Women's History*
- *Journal of World History*

<u>Web sites:</u>

- American History from the Library of Congress: <http://memory.loc.gov/ammem/>
- History Resources: <http://www.educationindex.com/history/>
- Internet Ancient History Sourcebook: <http://www.fordham.edu/halsall/ancient/asbook.html>
- Internet Modern History Sourcebook: <http://www.fordham.edu/halsall/mod/modsbook.html>
- University of Kentucky History Resources: <http://www.uky.edu/Subject/history.html>
- World History Archives: <http://www.hartford-hwp.com/archives/>

Journalism: <u>Journals:</u>

- American Journalism Review: <http://www.ajr.org/>
- Columbia Journalism Review: <http://www.cjr.org/>

Web site:

- University of Kentucky Journalism Resources: <http://www.uky.edu/Subject/journalism.html>

Law: Journals:

- *IDEA: The Journal of Law and Technology*
- *Intellectual Property*
- *Journal of Information Law and Technology*

Web sites:

- Law.com: <http://www.law.com/>
- Legal Information Institute, Cornell University: <http://www.law.cornell.edu/>
- WWW Virtual Library—Law: <http://www.law.indiana.edu/v-lib/>

Literature: Journals:

- *African-American Review*
- *Journal of Modern Literature*
- *PMLA*

Web sites:

- American Literature: <http://usinfo.org/oal/amlitweb.htm>
- English Literature: <http://www.english-literature.org/resources/>
- Online Literary Resources: <http://andromeda.rutgers.edu/~jlynch/Lit/>
- University of Washington E-Server: <http://eserver.org/>

Mathematics: Web sites:

- American Mathematics Society: <http://www.ams.org/>
- Catalog of Mathematics Resources on the WWW: <http://mthwww.uwc.edu/wwwmahes/files/math01.htm>
- MathSearch: <http://www.maths.usyd.edu.au/MS-freq-link.html>

Medicine: <u>Journals:</u>

- *JAMA: Journal of the American Medical Association:* <http://jama.ama-assn.org/>
- *New England Journal of Medicine:* <http://content.nejm.org/>

<u>Web sites:</u>

- Medscape: <http://www.medscape.com>
- Medweb: <http://www.medweb.emory.edu>
- National Institutes of Health: <http://www.nih.gov/>

Movies: <u>Journal:</u>

- *KINEMA: A Journal for Film and Audiovisual Media*

<u>Web site:</u>

- Internet Movie Database: <http://www.imdb.com/>

Music: <u>Journals:</u>

- *Journal of Musicology*
- *Musical Quarterly*

<u>Web sites:</u>

- Music Resources: <http://www2.siba.fi/ Kulttuuripalvelut/music.html>
- Worldwide Internet Music Resource: <http://www.music.indiana.edu/music_ resources/>

Philosophy: <u>Web sites:</u>

- Guide to Philosophy on the Internet: <http:// www.earlham.edu/~peters/philinks.htm# journals>
- Internet Encyclopedia of Philosophy: <http://www.iep.utm.edu/>>
- Philosophy Resources on the Internet: <http://www.epistemelinks.com/>
- Stanford Encyclopedia of Philosophy: <http://plato.stanford.edu/>

Physics: <u>Journals:</u>

- *Physical Review*
- *Physics Letters*

<u>Web sites:</u>

- About Physics Online: <http://physics.about.com/>
- PhysicsWeb: <http://physicsweb.org/>

Political Science: <u>Journals:</u>

- *The Americana*
- *Congressional Quarterly*
- *Foreign Affairs*
- *Harvard Political Review*
- *Political Science Quarterly*
- *Yale Political Monthly*

<u>Web sites:</u>

- Political Science Resources: <http://www.socsciresearch.com/r12.html>
- Political Science Resources on the Web: <http://www.lib.umich.edu/govdocs/polisci.html>

Psychology: <u>Journals:</u>

- *American Journal of Psychology*
- *Counseling Psychologist*
- *Journal of Personality and Social Psychology*
- *Psychological Review*

<u>Web sites:</u>

- Psychology Online Resource Central: <http://www.psych-central.com/>
- Psycho Web Resources: <http://www.psywww.com/>

Religion: <u>Journals:</u>

- *Cross Currents*
- *Religion and Literature*

Web sites:

- Iowa State University Religion Resources on the Web: <http://www.lib.iastate.edu/collections/eresourc/religion.html>
- Religion: Social Science Information Gateway: <http://sosig.ac.uk/welcome.html>

Sociology: Journals:

- *American Sociological Review*
- *Human Development and Family Life*
- *Journal of Sociology and Social Welfare*

Web sites:

- Socioweb: <http://www.socioweb.com/>

Theater: Web sites:

- Artslynx: International Arts Resources: Theater Resources: <http://www.artslynx.org/theatre/>
- University of Kentucky: World Wide Web Subject Catalog: Theater: <http://www.uky.edu/Subject/theater.html>
- WWW Virtual Library: Theater: <http://vl-theatre.com/>

Women's Studies: Journals:

- *Journal of Women's History*
- *Sister*
- *Womanist Theory and Research*
- *Women's Review of Books*

Web sites:

- University of York Library Women's Studies Internet Resources: <http://www.york.ac.uk/services/library/subjects/womenint.htm>
- Women's Studies (R)E-Sources on the Web: <http://scriptorium.lib.duke.edu/women/cyber.html>
- Women's Studies/Women's Issues Resources Sites: <http://www-unix.umbc.edu/~korenman/wmst/links.html>

36f   Taking notes

- **Working bibliography**   As you collect information, start a working bibliography that lists all the sources you will read. See section 37b on evaluating the citation before you spend time locating it. Some sources won't be as useful, and there are some questions you can ask yourself as you look at citations to see whether they belong in your working bibliography.

  Because you may not use all those sources in your paper, the final list of sources is likely to be shorter than the working bibliography. Make bibliographic entries on separate 3″ × 5″ cards so that you can easily insert new entries in alphabetical order. If you are using a computer, construct your list in a file that is separate from the paper. In each entry include all the information you will need in your bibliography. You may also want to include information you would need (such as the library call number for print sources) to find that source again. When you find a Web site or a document in an online database that you will be citing from, be sure to include the Web site address (the URL) or the database address and all the other relevant information you will need for the citation (see p. 198). That will save you time later on because you won't need to hunt up the document again. Many instructors also suggest that in your working bibliography you put the citation in correct bibliographic format (see Sections 40–44).

- **Note cards**   After you evaluate the source (see section 37) and decide that the information may be useful, record the information on note cards (either 3″ × 5″ or 4″ × 6″ cards) to summarize, paraphrase, or record a quotation (see section 38a). Use parentheses or brackets to record your thoughts as to how you can use this source in your paper. It is best to limit each note card to one short aspect of a topic so that you can reorder the cards later as you organize the whole project.

  Label the note card with the author's last name and shortened title, if needed, in the upper right-hand corner. Use a short phrase in the upper left-hand corner as a subject heading. As you write the information, include the exact page numbers and indicate to yourself whether the information is a summary, paraphrase, or quotation.

  If your instructor doesn't request note cards, you can put all this information in separate files on your computer and then print them out for use when you're writing your paper. Use the same short phrase you would have used in note cards for the titles of your files.

37

Evaluating Print and Internet Sources

We live in an age of information—such vast amounts of information that we cannot know everything about a subject. All of that information that comes streaming at us in newspapers, magazines, the media, books, journals, brochures, and Web sites is also of very uneven quality. People want to convince us to depend on their data, buy their products, accept their viewpoints, vote for their candidates, agree with their opinions, and rely on them as experts.

We sift and make decisions all the time about which information we will use based on how we evaluate the information. Evaluating sources, then, is a skill we need all the time, and applying that skill to research papers is equally important. Listed here are some stages in the process of evaluating sources.

37a Getting started

As you begin searching for information, ask yourself what kinds of information you are looking for and where you are likely to find appropriate sources for that kind of information. You want to be sure that you are headed in the right direction as you launch into your search, and this too is part of the evaluation process—evaluating where you are most likely to get the right kind of information for your purpose.

- **What kind of information are you looking for?**
  Do you want facts? opinions? news reports? research studies? analyses? historical accounts? personal reflections? data? public records? scholarly essays reflecting on the topic? reviews?

- **Where would you find such information?**
  Which sources are most likely to be useful? libraries with scholarly journals, books, and government publications? public libraries with popular magazines? the Internet? online databases in a library? newspapers? community records? someone on your campus?

  If, for example, you are searching for information on some current event, a reliable newspaper such as *The New York Times* will be a useful source, and it is likely to be available in a university library, a public library, and on the Web. If you need some statistics on the U.S. population, government census documents in libraries and on the Internet will be appropriate places to search (see 36d for Web addresses). But if you want to do research into local history, the archives of the local government offices and local newspaper are better places to start. Consider whether there are organizations designed to gather and publish the kinds of information you are seeking. And be sure to ask yourself if the organization's goal is to be objective or to gain support for its viewpoint.

37b Evaluating bibliographic citations

Before you spend time hunting for a source or read it, begin by looking at the following information in the citation to evaluate whether the source is worth finding or reading.

1. **Author**

   - *Credentials*
     - How reputable is the person (or organization) listed there?
     - What is the author's educational background?
     - What has the author written in the past about this topic?
     - Why is this person considered an expert or a reliable authority?

     You can learn more about the person by checking the Library of Congress (<http://lcweb.loc.gov>) to see what else the person has written, and the *Book Review Index* and *Book Review Digest* may lead you to reviews of other documents by this person. Your library may have citation indexes in the person's field that will lead you to other articles and short pieces by this person that have been cited by others. You can also use a search engine such as Google or Yahoo, or a metasearch engine such as Dogpile.com, to find Web sites that mention this person. (Common names, though, will turn up hundreds and hundreds of irrelevant results, so try to narrow the search by adding related terms.)

For biographical information you can read *Who's Who in America* or the *Biography Index*. There may also be information about the person in the publication such as listing of previous writings, awards, and notes about the author. Your goal is to get some sense of who this person is and why it's worth reading what that person wrote before you plunge in and begin reading. That may be important as you write the paper and build your case. For example, if you are citing a source to show the spread of AIDS in Africa, which of these sentences strengthens your argument?

"Dr. John Smith notes that the incidence of AIDS in Africa has more than doubled in the last five years."

(or)

"Dr. John Smith, head of the World Health Organization committee studying AIDS in African countries, notes that the incidence of AIDS in Africa has more than doubled in the last five years."

- *References*
  - Did a teacher or librarian or some other person who is knowledgeable about the topic mention this person?
  - Did you see the person listed in other sources that you've already determined to be trustworthy? When someone is an authority, you may find other references to this person. Or this person's viewpoint or perspective may be important to read.
  - If you found the source through a search engine listing, that has no relevance to how credible or worthwhile the source is. It merely means that the site contains words you used in your search term.

- *Institution or affiliation*
  - What organization, institution, or company is the person or Web site associated with?
  - What are the goals of this group?
  - Does the institution monitor or review what is published under its name?
  - Might this group be biased in some way? Are they trying to sell you something or convince you to accept their views? Do they conduct disinterested research?

-If you have the name of an institution, learn more about it by searching your library or the Internet.

2. **Timeliness**

- When was the source published? If it is important to get the most current information about your subject, decide if the source is outdated or not.
- Is the source a revision of an earlier edition? If so, it is likely to be more current, and a revision indicates that the source is sufficiently valuable to revise. Check the Internet, a library online catalog or *Books in Print* to see if you have the latest edition.
- Web site dates of origin or last revision are important, but that information might be difficult to find on the site. Look for the "last revised" date on the home page. Or try some of the links on the site. Older sites that have not been maintained are more likely to have many dead links that no longer work.

3. **Publisher/producer**

- Who published or produced the material?
- Is that publisher reputable? For example, a university press or a government agency is likely to be a reputable source that reviews what it publishes.
- Is the group recognized as being an authority?
- Is the publisher or group an appropriate one for this topic?
- Might the publisher be likely to have a particular bias? (For example, a brochure printed by an anti-abortion, right-to-life group is not going to argue for abortion.)
- Is there any review process or fact checking? (If a pharmaceutical company publishes data on a new drug it is developing, is there evidence of outside review of the data?)

4. **Audience**

- Can you tell who the intended audience is? Is that audience appropriate for your purposes?
- Is the material too specialized or too popular or brief to be useful? (A three-volume study of gene splitting is more than you need for a five-page paper on some genetically transmitted disease. But a half-page article on a visit to Antarctica won't tell you much about research into ozone depletion going on there.)

37c   Evaluating content

Print sources

When you have the source in hand, you can evaluate the content by keeping in mind the following important criteria:

- **Accuracy**   Are the facts accurate? Do they agree with other information you've read? Are there sources for the data given?

- **Comprehensiveness**   Is the topic covered in adequate depth? Or is it too superficial or limited to only one aspect that, therefore, overemphasizes only one part of the topic?

- **Credibility**   Is the source of the material generally considered trustworthy? Does the source have a review process or do fact checking? Is the author an expert? What are the author's credentials for writing about this topic?

- **Fairness**   If the author has a particular viewpoint, are differing views presented with some sense of fairness? Or are they presented as irrational or stupid?

- **Objectivity**   Is the language objective or emotional? Does the author acknowledge differing viewpoints? Are the various perspectives fairly presented? If you are reading an article in a magazine, do other articles in that source promote a particular viewpoint?

- **Relevance**   How closely related is the material to your topic? Is it really relevant or merely related? Is it too general or too specific? Too technical?

- **Timeliness**   Is the information current enough to be useful? How necessary is timeliness for your topic?

To help you determine the degree to which the criteria listed above are present in the source, try the following:

- Read the preface. What does the author want to accomplish?

- Browse through the table of contents and the index. Is the topic covered in enough depth to be helpful?

- Is there a list of references that look as if the author has consulted other sources and that may lead you to useful related material?

- Are you the intended audience? Consider the tone, style, level of information, and assumptions the author makes about the reader. Are they appropriate to your needs?

- Is the content of the source fact, opinion, or propaganda? If the material is presented as factual, are the sources of the facts clearly indicated? Do you think there's enough evidence offered? Is the coverage comprehensive? (As you learn more about the topic, you will notice that this gets easier as you become more of an expert.) Is the language emotional or objective?

- Are there broad, sweeping generalizations that overstate or simplify the matter?

- Does the author use a mix of primary and secondary sources?

- To determine accuracy, consider whether the source is out-dated. Do some cross-checking. Do you find some of the same information elsewhere?

- Are there arguments that are one-sided with no acknowledgement of other viewpoints?

Internet sources

Evaluating Internet sources is particularly difficult because anyone can put up anything he or she wants to on the Internet. There is no way to monitor or to check facts, though there are some site ratings you can check. At the end of the essay by Hope Tillman (listed on p. 158), you will find a discussion of various ratings given to sites by companies that issue awards (some of which are objective ratings for quality and some of which are merely to promote the company issuing the award).

Some criteria to consider as you read Internet sources:

1. **Authorship**

   -*Is there an author or organization clearly indicated?*
   If so, review the questions about authorship listed in 37b. Can the author be contacted?
   -*What can you find out about the author?*
   If there is no information on the site, use a search engine or search Usenet for the person. You may find the author's home page or other documents that mention this person. If the person is associated with a university, look at the university Web site.

*-If there is an organization sponsoring the page, what can
you learn about the organization and who they are?*
You can search the site by following links to the
home page or going back a previous level on the site
by deleting the last part of the address, after the
various "/" marks. Or try contacting the person who
maintains the site if a name, title, or e-mail address
is included. Or there may be a "contact us" link to
which you can send an e-mail.

Does the organization take responsibility for
what's on the site? Does it monitor or review what's
there? Look at the address. If it ends in ".edu," that
indicates it's an educational institution. If it ends in
".gov," whatever you find should be fairly objective
government-sponsored material. Addresses with
".org" are usually nonprofit organizations that are
advocacy groups. For example, the Sierra Club, at
<http://www.sierraclub.org>, is an advocacy group
whose postings will conform to their goals of
environmental protection. Information posted by
advocacy groups may be accurate but not entirely
objective. If the site has a ".com" address, it's more
likely to be promoting or selling something.

2. **Accuracy of information**

   -Is there documentation to indicate the source of the
   information? There may be a link to the original
   source of the information.
   -Can you tell how well researched the information is?
   -Are criteria for including information offered?
   -Is there a bibliography or links to other useful sites?
   Has the author considered information on those sites
   or considered viewpoints represented there?
   -Is the information current? When was it updated?
   (Check at the bottom of the page for a "last revised"
   date. If there are numerous dead links, that's a clue
   that the page has not been updated recently.)
   -Is there an indication of bias on the site?
   -Does the site have any credentials such as being rated
   by a reputable rating group? If you see a high
   rating, is that because of the reliability of the
   content or the quality of the graphics? (An
   attractive page is not a reason for accepting its
   information as reliable.)

3. **Goals of the site**

-What is the purpose of the site? advertise? persuade?
   provide information? provide disinformation? For
   example, some groups intent on helping their
   candidate get elected put up sites that emphasize the
   opponent's weaknesses or that ridicule the opponent.
   Some sites are owned by hate groups that manage to
   disguise their real purpose, and some sites appear to
   be objective but are promoting some product or service.
-Are the goals of the site clearly indicated?
-Who is the intended audience?
-Is there a lot of flash and color and gimmicks to attract
   attention? Is that masking a lack of sound
   information or a blatant attempt to get you to buy or
   do something?

4. **Access**

-How did you find the site? Were there links from
   reputable sites? from ads? If you found the site
   through a search engine, that means only that the
   site has the keywords in your search term
   prominently placed or used with great frequency. It
   could also mean that the site owner paid to be listed
   at or near the top of the results list. If sites are
   prominently listed because they have paid to be seen
   on the results lists, they are sometimes identified as
   "sponsored links." If you found the site by browsing
   through a subject directory, that may mean only that
   someone at that site registered it with that directory.

Internet Resources on Evaluation

Some Web sites that have useful materials on evaluating
sources and links to other useful sites are the following:

- Barker, Joe, and Saifon Obromsook. "Evaluating Web
  Pages": <http://www.lib.berkeley.edu/TeachingLib/
  Guides/Internet/Evaluate.html>

- Engle, Michael. "Evaluating Web Sites: Criteria and Tools":
  <http://www.library.cornell.edu/okuref/research/
  webeval.html>

- Harris, Robert. "Evaluating Internet Research Sources":
  <http://www.virtualsalt.com/evalu8it.htm>

- Henderson, John R. "The ICYouSee Critical Thinking Guide": <http://www.ithaca.edu/library/training/think.html>

- Kirk, Elizabeth. "Evaluating Information Found on the Internet": <http://www.library.jhu.edu/elp/useit/evaluate/index.html>

- Richmond, Betsy. "Ten C's for Evaluating Internet Resources": <http://www.uwec.edu/library/Guides/tencs.html>

- Smith, Alastair. "Criteria for Evaluation of Internet Information Sources": <http://www.vuw.ac.nz/~agsmith/evaln/index.htm>

- Tillman, Hope. "Evaluating Quality on the Net": <http://www.hopetillman.com/findqual.html>

- UCLA Biomed Library. "Searching for and Evaluating Web Resources": <http://www.library.ucla.edu/libraries/biomed/tutorials/searchweb.html>

38

Integrating Sources

As you write your paper, you will be including material from the sources you found during your research. As you include those sources, you have several important writing tasks:

- You have to help the reader see why the source is being quoted or referred to so that the reader sees the relevance (see 38a).

- Because you may also be incorporating summaries, paraphrases, and quotations, you need to be able to distinguish between them. It is also important to weave these in smoothly and to distinguish for the reader as to whether you are summarizing, paraphrasing, or quoting (see 38b and 38c).

- A very useful way to integrate references to source material, summaries, paraphrases, and quotations is to signal your reader by using signal words (see 38d) to introduce and smoothly blend these sources into your writing.

- Finally, as you use sources in your writing, you want to be sure that you are not plagiarizing the material (see 38e).

38a   Showing the relevance

Suppose you read a paragraph that dealt with genetically modified foods and saw the following two sentences:

> Biologists are working toward developing a strain of corn that can withstand drought. Gerritson notes that the drought in Africa will most likely continue through this decade (81).

Did it take you a moment to figure out the connection? The writer of those sentences failed to help us see the relevance of the second sentence. The sentence was just dropped in, and the reader was left to figure out the point being made.
Notice the difference in this revised version:

> **Revised:**   Biologists are working toward developing a strain of corn that can withstand drought. This will be needed in the near future because, as Gerritson notes, the drought in Africa will most likely continue through this decade (81).

The revised version adds an explanation to the reader as to how the source material is connected to the rest of the paragraph. One way to check that you have integrated a source effectively is to ask yourself if you have explained the relevance of the material you are including. Put the explanation before the source material so that the reader can move forward easily.
Here's another example in which a quotation is dropped awkwardly in a paragraph:

> Marketing research has shown that college-bound first-year students spend millions in furnishing their residence hall rooms. "Milgrim will be launching a funky line of colorful bedding exclusively for Hines" (27), says Feliz Morrano, design coordinator at Hines.

Does this revised version clarify that quotation?

> **Revised:**   Marketing research has shown that college-bound first-year students spend millions in furnishing

their residence hall rooms. To cash in on this market, large discount chains are eager to introduce the work of well-known clothing designers such as Tom Milgrim. For example, Feliz Morrano, design coordinator at Hines, a major discount retailer, recently announced that "Milgrim will be launching a funky line of colorful bedding exclusively for Hines" (27).

38b Writing summaries and paraphrases

As you gather information from your sources, you may need to summarize or paraphrase them when you include them in your writing.

1. Summaries

> A summary is a brief statement of the main idea in a source, using your own words. Include a citation to the source.

Characteristics of summaries:
- Are written in your own words
- Include only the main points, omitting details, facts, examples, illustrations, direct quotations, and other specifics
- Use fewer words than the source
- Do not have to be in the same order as the source
- Are objective and do not include your own interpretation

Good reasons for using summaries are that the source has unnecessary detail, that the writing is not particularly memorable or worth quoting, or that you want to keep your writing concise.

2. Paraphrases

> A paraphrase restates the information from a source, using your own words. Include a citation to the source.

Characteristics of paraphrases:
- Have approximately the same number of words as the source
- Include all main points and important details in the source

- Use your own words, not those of the source
- Keep the same organization as the source
- Are more detailed than a summary
- Are objective and do not include your interpretation

38c Using quotations

> A quotation is the record of the exact words of a written or spoken source and is set off by quotation marks. All quotations should have citation to the source.

Guidelines for using quotations:

- Use quotations as evidence, support, or further explanation of what you have written. Quotations are not substitutes for stating your point in your own words.

- Before you include the quotation, indicate the point the quotation is making and why that quotation is relevant.

- Use quotations sparingly. Too many quotations strung together with little of your own writing can make a paper look like a scrapbook of pasted-together sources, not a thoughtful integration of what is known about a subject.

- Use quotations that illustrate an authority's viewpoint or style or that would not be as effective if rewritten in different words.

- Introduce quotations with signal words (see 38d).

  For guidelines on punctuating quotations, see section 22.

38d Using signal words with sources

As you include summaries, paraphrases, and quotations in your papers, you need to integrate them smoothly so that there is no sudden jump or break between the flow of your words and the source material. Use the following strategies to prepare your readers and to create that needed smooth transition into the inserted material:

- **Use signal phrases**
  Signal words or phrases let the reader know a quotation will follow. Choose a phrase or word that is appropriate to

the quotation and indicates the relationship to the ideas being discussed.

In 1990 when the United Nations International Human Rights Commission *predicted* "there will be an outburst of major violations of human rights in Yugoslavia within the next few years" (14), few people in Europe or the United States paid attention to the warning. (United Nations International Human Rights Commission. *The Future of Human Rights in Eastern Europe*. New York: United Nations, 1990.)

SOME COMMON SIGNAL WORDS

according to	considers	observes
acknowledges	denies	points out
admits	describes	predicts
argues	disagrees	proposes
asserts	emphasizes	rejects
comments	explains	reports
complains	finds	responds
concedes	insists	suggests
concludes	maintains	thinks
condemns	notes warns	

- **Explain the connection with signal words**
  Do not let the quotation make a point by itself. Explain to your reader what the quotation indicates or adds to your explanation or argument. When you explain the connection between a quotation you use and the point you are making, you are showing the logical link. If it is appropriate, you can add a follow-up comment that continues to integrate the quotation into your paragraph.

  ### Quotation not integrated into the paragraph:
  Modern farming techniques are different from those used twenty years ago. John Hession, an Iowa soybean grower, says, "Without a computer program to plan my crop allotments or to record my expenses, I'd be back in the dark ages of guessing what to do." New computer software programs are being developed commercially and are selling well.
  (Hession, John. Personal interview. 27 July 2005.)

  The quotation here is abruptly dropped into the paragraph, without an introduction and without a clear indication from the writer as to how Mr. Hession's statement fits into the ideas being discussed.

Revised:

Modern farming techniques differ from those of twenty years ago, *particularly in the use of computer programs for planning and budgeting.* John Hession, an Iowa soybean grower *who relies heavily on computers, confirms this* when he notes, "Without a computer program to plan my crop allotments or to record my expenses, I'd be back in the dark ages of guessing what to do." Commercial software programs *such as those used by Mr. Hession, for crop allotments and budgeting,* are being developed and are selling well.

The added words in italics explain how Mr. Hession's statement confirms the point being made.

38e Avoiding plagiarism

Plagiarism results when writers fail to document a source so that the words and ideas of someone else are presented as the writer's own work.

- **Why is avoiding plagiarism important?**

  Citing someone else's work as your own (that is, failing to acknowledge your source by failing to cite it) is a form of stealing, both from yourself and others. Plagiarizing instead of learning when and how to cite sources robs you of the opportunity to learn how to do it. Because learning how to cite sources is complicated, it does take time to learn, and writing research papers is an excellent opportunity to get such practice. Plagiarizing also robs the writer of the pleasure that writers feel when they find new information on their own. Because plagiarism is stealing the work of others without giving them credit, it's also an illegal act. Some colleges and universities have penalties for plagiarizing that can cause a student to fail the course, be suspended, or be dismissed from the college. And numerous software programs and Internet sites help instructors identify plagiarized materials. Later on, out in the world of work, there have been numerous cases where reporters and others have been publicly identified as plagiarizing and have lost jobs and probably their careers as well. For example, a president of a New England college who did not acknowledge his sources in some of his public writing was forced to retire. Plagiarism is also unethical as well as illegal because without lists of sources, others who are interested in learning more from your sources are robbed of the opportunity to find and read them.

So, for numerous reasons, all writers want to avoid plagiarism. But some writers plagiarize unintentionally when they don't realize they should be documenting some sources they are using or when they haven't collected information properly and don't recognize information in their notes that they copied from others. Unintentional plagiarism, however, can still result in the same penalties as intentional plagiarism.

hint

Avoiding Plagiarism

To avoid plagiarism, read over your paper and ask yourself whether your readers can properly identify which ideas and words are yours and which are from the sources you cite. If that is clear, then you are not plagiarizing.

hint

Some Types of Plagiarism

Plagiarism occurs in several different ways:

- Using the exact words of someone without putting those words in quotation marks and without citing the source.

- Changing the words of another person into your own words by paraphrasing or summarizing without citing the source.

- Stating ideas or research specifically attributed to another person or persons without citing the source.

- Claiming authorship of a paper written by someone else.

- Not being able to distinguish information that needs to be documented from common knowledge that does not need to be documented. Plagiarism results when the writer thinks something is common knowledge even though it isn't and fails to document it.

- **What information needs to be documented?**
  When we use the ideas, findings, data, conclusions, arguments, and words of others, we need to acknowl-

edge that we are borrowing their work and inserting it in our own by documenting. Consciously or unconsciously passing off the work of others as our own results in the very serious form of stealing known as plagiarism, an act that has serious consequences for the writer who plagiarizes.

If you summarize, paraphrase, or use the words of someone else (see 38b), you need to provide documentation for those sources.

- **What information does not need to be documented?**

Common knowledge, that body of general ideas we share with our readers, does not have to be documented. Common knowledge consists of the following:

- Standard information on a subject that your readers know
- Information that is widely shared and can be found in numerous sources

For example, it is common knowledge among most Americans aware of current energy problems that solar power is one answer to future energy needs. But forecasts about how widely solar power may be used in twenty years or estimates of the cost-effectiveness of using solar energy would be the work of some person or group studying the subject, and documentation would be needed. Similarly, it is common knowledge that too many people are seriously overweight, but specific statistics collected by some researcher or group is not common knowledge and needs to be cited.

Field research you conduct also does not need to be documented, though you should indicate that you are reporting your own findings.

Original source:

Researchers studying human aggression are discovering that, in contrast to the usual stereotypes, patterns of aggression among girls and women under some circumstances may mirror or even exaggerate those seen in boys and men. And while women's weapons are often words, fists may be used too.

—Abigail Zuger, "A Fistful of Hostility Is Found in Women." *The New York Times* 28 Jul. 1998, B9.

Plagiarized version:

Women can be as hostile as men. According to Abigail Zuger, researchers studying human aggression are discovering that, in contrast to the usual stereotypes, patterns of aggression among girls and women under some circumstances may mirror or even exaggerate those seen in boys and men. And while women's weapons are often words, fists may be used too (B9).

Revision:

An acceptable revision of the plagiarized version above would have either a paraphrase or summary in the writer's own words or would indicate, with quotation marks, the exact words of the source. (See 38a.)

---

hint

ESL: Citing Sources

In some cultures, educated writers are expected to know and incorporate the thinking of great scholars. It may be considered an insult to the reader to mention the names of the scholars, implying that the reader is not educated enough to recognize the references. However, in American writing, this is not the case, and writers are always expected to acknowledge their sources and give public credit to the source.

39

Designing Documents

As we write, we think about the words and ideas we are composing and the grammatical correctness of the language used. But in an age of so much visual communication, we also have to be concerned with the visual presentation of our writing. This is necessary because readers need clear visual markers to help understand the information on the page and because we want readers to read our documents. When readers see overcrowded pages with little white space and long, unbroken sections of text, they are likely to react negatively. This section will offer guidelines for paper presentation and for ways to make your writing more visually effective. For suggestions for how to make your documents visually effective, see 39b.

39a   Paper presentation

Your instructor may request that you follow specific guide-lines for papers in that course. But if not, you can follow these general guidelines:

Paper: Use 8 1/2″ × 11″ white, unlined paper. Print out or write on one side only.

Line spacing: Double-space throughout, including every line in the title, the text of the paper, headings, quotations, and bibliography.

Margins: Allow one inch at the top and bottom and at both sides of the page, but put page numbers one-half inch from the top at the right side of the page. Justify margins at the left, but not at the right side of the page.

Indentation: Indent the first line of every paragraph one-half inch or five spaces from the left margin. For long quotations within paragraphs, indent one inch or ten spaces from the left margin.

Title: For MLA format, research papers and reports do not need a title page unless your instructor asks for one. If you don't need a title page, leave a margin of one inch from the top, and then on separate lines, double-spaced, at the left side of the page, put your name, your instructor's name, the course number, and date submitted. Then, double-space and type the paper title, centered on the page. If a second line is needed, double-space between lines. Then double-space between the title and the first line of your paper. For APA format, the title page includes an abbreviated title and page number one-half inch from the top of the page, at the upper left-hand corner. The title is centered and double-spaced in the middle of the page, with your name, instructor's name, course number, and date double-spaced and centered under the title.

Page ordering: For MLA format, start with the first page with the title, then the text, and then end notes on a separate page, with the Works Cited (on a separate page) at the end. For APA format, place the title page first and then the text of the paper. Following that, starting on separate pages for each, put references, appendices, footnotes, tables, figure captions, and at the end, figures (each on a separate page).

Font: Use ten- to twelve-point type and a standard font with serifs, such as Helvetica, Times New Roman, or

Palatino. Do not use fonts that resemble cursive writing, that do not have serifs, or that are unusually shaped and difficult to read.

Headings and subheadings: These are short titles that define sections and subsections in long reports or papers. They provide visual emphasis by breaking the paper into manageable portions that are easily seen and identified. For MLA format, put top-level headings in boldface type, capitalized (except for short prepositions and articles), and centered on the page. Second-level headings for subsections are boldfaced at the left margin, with only the first word capitalized. For APA, one level of heading is recommended for short papers, centered on the page, with each word capitalized (except short prepositions and articles that are not the first word of the heading title).

Visuals: For MLA, place visuals at the point in the text where the reader may benefit by consulting them. Be sure to include a caption that explains the chart, table, diagram, or graph. In APA, all visuals are placed on separate pages, at the end of the paper, with tables first and then figures. (See 39b for more on visuals.)

39b Visual elements

Visual appearance has always been important, but it is becoming even more so because people are regularly being overloaded with a great deal of information. To get our readers' attention, we have to present them with attractive pages and help them get through the documents we give them. And we can condense some information and make it clearer with visual elements such as lists, graphs, and tables. We aren't all artists, but we have the technological tools to word process and have our writing printed out neatly and attractively. With a few basic principles in mind, we can produce documents that our readers find attractive and readable.

Include white space. Well-used white space on the page invites readers into the page and offers some relief from the heaviness of blocks of print. Leave open space around margins and between sections of a document. Indent where it's appropriate, and add other visuals such as photographs and color.

Use headings and subheadings. Announce new topics or segments of a topic, especially in long essays and reports.

Use lists wherever possible. Instead of long paragraphs discussing many related items, group the items in lists with bullets, dashes, or numbers. This also adds white space, especially if you indent the list.

Use contrast to add emphasis. Show differences between elements and indicate more important from less important elements with a few different type sizes, indentations, graphics, and background shading. Boldface type can also help, but don't overdo it so that the page looks darker and more cluttered.

Use visuals such as tables and charts. Tables and charts can convey information easily and succinctly.

Tables

Tables present information in columns and rows and can include numbers or words. (See Table 39–1.)

Visuals

To present data in visual form, you can also use various kinds of figures, such as pie charts (especially for percentages or fractions of a whole), bar graphs and line graphs (especially for comparative data or change over time), images (such as diagrams, drawings, and photographs), and flowcharts (to help readers follow a process or show options in making decisions). (See Figures 1 and 2 on p. 170.)

Use appendixes for detailed information. In documents with detailed information such as tables, figures, questionnaires, lists, photographs, cost estimates, and so on, don't interrupt the flow of the document by including such

(continued on p. 171)

TABLE 39-1		
Expectation	**Women**	**Men**
Starting salary	$49,190	$55,950
Signing bonus an important factor	31%	42%
Signing bonus expected	27%	51%
Signing bonus expectation	$7,000	$7,900
Year end bonus an important factor	38%	47%
Year end bonus expected	33%	49%
Year end bonus expectation	$8,400	$13,300
Health insurance an important factor	72%	52%
Entrepreneurial environment preferred	35%	55%
Stock option an important factor	33%	46%

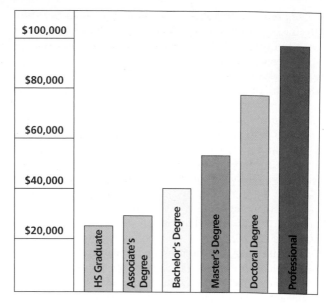

FIGURE 1 Average Annual Personal Income in the United States.

Source: "The Value of a College Education." Rev. 9 October 2001. Abilene Christian University. 15 June 2005 <http://www.acu.edu/admissions/ugrad/yei/ed-value.html>. Reprinted with permission.

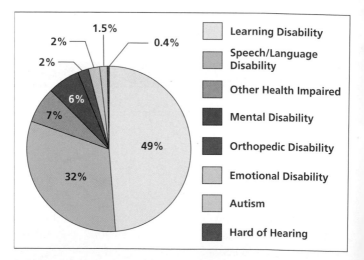

FIGURE 2 Percentage of Disability Categories.

Source: U.S. Department of Education. Improve Student Performance: Successful Practices for Students with Disabilities 2004 Summer Workshop Presentation by Rick Woodford.

material there. Instead, move the information to appendixes (you can have more than one) so that readers who
do not need that data can skip it. Refer to each appendix
in your document. If you have only one appendix, label it
"Appendix." If you have more than one, label them
"Appendix A," "Appendix B," and so on. Give each appendix a title.

Avoid busy, cluttered pages. Although you want your
documents to have variety and interest, you also have to
avoid creating pages that are too busy and cluttered. That
can happen when there are too many different font types
and sizes and too much use of boldface or italics. Try to
limit your fonts to two or, at most, three different ones.

VIII
Documentation

....

Contents of this section

QUESTION & CORRECT

This part contains sections with information on documenting your sources in your paper, in endnotes or footnotes, and in the list of works cited (or references) at the end of the paper. The formats for MLA, APA, *Chicago Manual of Style* (CM), and Council of Science Editors (CSE) are explained and illustrated. Indexes to the examples for the notes and bibliographies will lead you to the ones you need, and there is also a list of style manuals for fields that use other documentation formats.

When you research a topic, you are building on the work of others, and your work, in turn, contributes to the pool of knowledge about the topic for others who will read and depend on your research. Thus, it is necessary to give credit to those whose work you use and to document your sources so completely that readers of your work can find the sources you used.

Documentation formats vary, depending on the field of study. Organizations such as newspapers and other publishing companies, businesses, and large organizations often have their own formats that are explained in their style manuals (see section 44).

40

···

MLA Style

For English and other humanities, use the format of the Modern Language Association (MLA):

> Gibaldi, Joseph. *MLA Handbook for Writers of Research Papers*. 6th ed. New York: MLA, 2003.

Some of the major features of MLA style are as follows:

- For in-text citations, give the author's last name (if you haven't mentioned the name in the sentence) and the page number of the source, preferably within the sentence rather than after it.

- Use full first and last names and middle initials of authors.

- Capitalize all major words in titles, and underline titles or put them in italics. Enclose article titles in quotation marks.

- In the Works Cited list at the end of the paper, give full publication information, alphabetized by author.

Three Aspects of MLA Format to Consider

- **In-text citations**
  In your paper you need parenthetical references to your sources to acknowledge wherever you use the words, ideas, and facts you've taken from your sources.
- **Endnotes**
  If you need to add material that would disrupt your paper if it were included in the text, include such notes at the end of the paper.
- **Works Cited list**
  At the end of your paper, include a list of the sources from which you have quoted, summarized, or paraphrased.

40a In-text citations

The purpose of in-text citations is to help your reader find the appropriate reference in the list of works cited at the end of the paper. Current MLA format recommends parenthetical references (not footnotes), depending on how much information you include in your sentence or in your introduction to a quotation. Try to be brief, but not at the expense of clarity, and remember to use signal words and phrases (see 38d).

Index to Examples of MLA In-text Citations

1. **Author's name in the text**
   If the author's name is mentioned in a sentence, only the page number is needed in parentheses. Try to put the reference where there is a natural pause so that the flow of the sentence is not interrupted. A natural pause is often at the end of the sentence.

   > In Nathaniel Coplin's essay, he argues that Pitlow was not aware of his Cherokee heritage (27).

2. **Author's name not in the text**
   If the author's name is not in your sentence, put the last name in parentheses, leave a space with no punctuation, and then put the page number.

   > Recent research on sleep and dreaming indicates that dreams move backward in time as the night progresses (Dement 72).

3. **Two or more works by the same author**
   If you used two or more different sources by the same author, put a comma after the author's last name and include a shortened version of the title followed by the page reference. If the author's name is in the text, include only the title and page reference.

   > One current theory emphasizes the principle that dreams express "profound aspects of personality" (Foulkes, <u>Sleep</u> 144). Foulkes' investigation shows that young children's dreams are "rather simple and unemotional" ("Children's Dreams" 90).

4. **Two or three authors**
   If your source has two or three authors, either name them in your sentence or include the names in parentheses.

   > Jeffrey and Milanovitch argue that the recently reported statistics for teenage pregnancies are inaccurate (112).

   > (or)

   > The recently reported statistics for teenage pregnancies are said to be inaccurate (Jeffrey and Milanovitch 112).

5. **More than three authors**
   If your source has more than three authors, either use the first author's last name followed by "et al." (which means "and others") or list all the last names.

The conclusions drawn from a survey on the growth of the Internet, conducted by Martin et al., are that global usage will double within two years (36).

(or)

Recent figures on the growth of the Internet indicate that global usage will double within two years (Martin, Ober, Mancuso, and Blum 36).

6. **Authors with the same last name**
When two different authors have the same last name and their names are used in the paragraph, include each person's first name every time the name is included. When the names are not included in the text, use the first intial of each person's name in parentheses.

As Gay Lynn Smith states, language and vocabulary are part of any curriculum, and the arts hold a language all their own (61). Agreeing with this view, Shawn Smith concludes that schools that only teach the process of art production may, in fact, be doing more harm than good. Clearly, as Shawn Smith explains, teachers need time to teach students the value of art dialogue (41).

Language and vocabulary are part of any curriculum, and the arts hold a language all their own (G. Smith 61). Schools that only teach the process of art production, may, in fact, be doing more harm than good. Clearly, teachers need time to teach students the value of art dialogue (S. Smith 41).

7. **Unknown author**
If the author is unknown, use a shortened form of the title in your citation.

More detailed nutritional information in food labels is proving to be a great advantage to diabetics ("New Labeling Laws" 3).

8. **Reference after a quotation**
A reference directly after a quotation follows outside the quotation mark but before the period.

Advertising has been described as "shouting at the masses" (Newelt 90).

9. **The Bible and other sacred texts**
   When religious texts are cited in sentences, include the title of the book and as much locator information as possible (for example, Genesis 29.6). But when the reference is in parentheses, the title of the book is often abbreviated (for example, Gen. 29.6).

   > When Jacob travels to Haran, he stops at a well where Rachel has come to water her flock (Gen. 29.6).

10. **Page number unknown**
    If your document has no page numbers, cite only the author's name.

    > Although still in its infancy, seismic research ultimately may have important applications for elephant conservation and even for human health (Shwartz).

11. **Corporate author or government document**
    Use the name of the corporation or government agency, shortened or in full. It is better to include long names in your sentence to avoid extending the parenthetical reference.

    > The United Nations Regional Flood Containment Commission has been studying weather patterns that contribute to flooding in Africa (4).

12. **Entire work**
    For an entire work, it is preferable to include the author's name in the text.

    > Lafmun was the first to argue that small infants respond to music.

13. **Multivolume work**
    When you cite a source from a multivolume work, put the volume number first, then a colon, then a space, and then the page number. Do not use the word "volume" or "page."

    > In his <u>History of the Civil War</u>, Jimmersen traces the economic influences that contributed to the decisions of several states to stay in the Union (3: 798-823).

14. **Reference work**
    For material from a reference work with no author for the entry cited, include a shortened version of the title,

beginning with the word by which it is alphabetized in the Works Cited list.

> The Doppler effect is the apparent difference between the frequency at which sound or light waves leave a source and that at which they reach an observer, caused by relative motion of the observer and the wave source ("Doppler" 182)

15. **Work in an anthology**
Cite the name of the author of the work, not the editor of the anthology, in the sentence or in parentheses.

> When Millet refers to her childhood, she uses vague references such as "in my younger days" (14) rather than specific ages or dates.

16. **Literary work**
For classic prose works, such as novels or plays available in several editions, it is helpful to provide more information than a page reference to the edition you used. A book, part, or chapter number might help readers locate the reference in any copy. Give the page number first, add a semicolon, and then give other identifying information, using the abbreviations "bk." for "book," "pt." for "part," and "ch." for "chapter."

> In The Prince, Machiavelli reminds us that although some manage to jump from humble origins to great power, such people find their greatest challenge to be staying in power: "Those who rise from private citizens to be princes merely by fortune have little trouble in rising but very much trouble in maintaining their position" (23; ch. 7).

> In <u>Anna Karenina</u>, Leo Tolstoy concludes the novel with Levin's thoughts about how meaning has entered his life:
> > But my whole life, every moment of my life, independent of whatever may happen to me, will be, not meaningless as before, but full of the deep meaning which I shall have the power to impress upon it. (700; pt. 8; ch. 19)

For verse plays and poems, omit page numbers and cite by division (act, scene, canto, etc.) and line, with periods separating the various numbers. For lines, initially use the word "line" or "lines" and then afterward, give the numbers alone.

> Eliot again reminds us of society's superficiality in "The Love Song of J. Alfred Prufrock": "There will be time, there will be time / To prepare a face to meet the faces that you meet" (lines 26-27).

17. **Verse play**

For verse plays, include the act, scene, and line numbers, with periods between each.

> Shakespeare's ambition-driven Lady Macbeth advises her husband: "Look like th' innocent flower, / But be the serpent under 't" (<u>Mac</u>. 1.5.65-66).

18. **Poem**

For a poem that is divided into parts, cite the part and line numbers, separated by a period. For poems not divided into parts, use the word "line" or "lines" and not an abbreviation (which might be confused with a number).

a) A poem that is divided into parts ("The Rime of the Ancient Mariner" by Samuel Taylor Coleridge):

> He holds him with his glittering eye—
>   The Wedding-Guest stood still,
> And listens like a three years' child:
>   The Mariner hath his will. (1.13-16)

b) A poem that is not divided into parts ("Jabberwocky" by Lewis Carroll):

> "Beware the Jabberwock, my son!
>   The jaws that bite, the claws that catch!
> Beware the Jubjub bird, and shun
>   The frumious Bandersnatch!" (lines 5-8)

19. **More than one work in a parenthetical reference**

When you have more than one reference to include within a single set of parentheses, cite each work as you normally would and use a semicolon between the entries. Don't overload the reference with too many names. If you need to include a number of citations, cite them in a note.

> Several biographers explain that they have not been able to account for his life in the long period between his first and second novels (Diltonal 244; Van Leeven 43; Jillenwok 171).

20. **Indirect source**
    If you have to rely on a secondhand source in which
    someone's quoted words appear in a source written by
    someone else, start the citation with the abbreviation
    "qtd. in."

    > Although Newman has established a high degree of
    > accuracy for such tests, he reminds us that "no test
    > like this is ever completely and totally accurate" (qtd.
    > in Mazor 33).

21. **Electronic sources**
    For electronic sources, start with the word by which the
    source is alphabetized in your Works Cited list (see 40c).

    > The World Wide Web is a helpful source for
    > community groups seeking information on how to
    > protest projects that damage the local environment
    > ("Environmental Activism").

22. **Personal communication, interview, lecture, speech**
    Enclose in parentheses the name of the person whom
    you interviewed or heard speak. That will lead your
    reader to the right bibliographic citation in the Works
    Cited list.

    > The most urgent reason for the increase in the
    > budget was soaring costs of energy (Van Leeuk).

40b Endnotes

When you have additional comments or information that
would disrupt the paper, cite the information in endnotes
numbered consecutively throughout the paper. Put the number at the end of the phrase, clause, or sentence containing
the material you are referring to. Use a superscript (raised)
number above the line, with no punctuation. Leave no extra
space before the number and one extra space after it, whether
it appears in the middle of the sentence or at the end.

> The treasure hunt for sixteenth-century pirate loot
> buried in Nova Scotia began in 1927,[3] but hunting was
> discontinued when the treasure seekers found the site
> flooded at high tide.[4]

At the end of your paper, begin a new sheet with the
heading "Notes" (neither underlined nor in quotation
marks). Leave a one-inch margin at the top, center the

heading, double-space, and then begin listing your notes. For each note, indent five spaces (or one-half inch), use a superscript (raised) number, and begin the note. Double-space, and if the note continues on the next line, begin that line at the left margin. The format is slightly different from that used in the Works Cited section in that the author's name appears in normal order, followed by a comma, the title, publisher and date in parentheses, and a page reference.

[3]Some historians argue that this widely accepted date is inaccurate. See Jerome Flynn, <u>Buried Treasures</u> (New York: Newport, 1978) 29-43.

[4]Avery Jones and Jessica Lund, "The Nova Scotia Mystery Treasure," <u>Contemporary History</u> 9 (1985): 81-83.

If you are asked to use footnotes instead of endnotes, place them at the bottoms of pages, beginning four lines (two double spaces) below the text. Single-space footnotes, but double-space between them. Number them consecutively throughout the paper.

40c Works Cited list

The Works Cited list includes all the sources cited in your paper, not other materials you read but didn't refer to. Arrange the list alphabetically by the last name of the author, and if there is no author, alphabetize by the first word of the title, but not the articles <u>A</u>, <u>An</u>, or <u>The</u> if the article is the first needed word in the title. Omit the article if it is not needed.

For the Works Cited section, begin a new sheet of paper, leave a one-inch margin at the top, center the heading "Works Cited" (neither underlined nor in quotation marks), and then double-space before the first entry. For each entry, begin at the left margin for the first line and indent five spaces (or one-half inch) for additional lines in the entry. Double-space throughout. Place the Works Cited list at the end of your paper after the Notes list, if you have one.

Books: There are three main parts of a book citation: (1) name of the author, (2) title of the book, and (3) publishing information. Each part is followed by a period and a space, and all lines after are indented five spaces.

Book

Last name of author, comma, first name, period

Williams, Robin.

Title of book underlined, period

The Non-Designer's Design Book.

Place of publication, colon, shortened name of publisher, comma, year of publication, period

Berkeley: Peachpit, 1994.

Articles in Periodicals: There are three main parts of a journal article citation: (1) name of the author, (2) title of the article and the journal, and (3) publishing information, which includes volume number of the periodical, date of publication, and page numbers.

Journal

Last name of author, comma, first name, period

Rogers, Pat.

Title of article in quotation marks, period, journal title underlined

"Why Trivia? Myth, Etymology, and Topography." Arion

Volume number, date of publication in parentheses, colon, pages, period

12 (2005): 144-54.

There are three main parts of a magazine article citation: (1) name of the author, (2) title of the article and the magazine, and (3) date of publication and page numbers.

Magazine

> Last name, comma, first name of author, period
>
> > Lizza, Ryan.

> Title of article in quotation marks, period, journal title underlined
>
> > "White House Watch: Charles at Large." <u>The New Republic</u>

> Day, month (abbreviated), period, year, colon, pages, period
>
> > 25 Apr. 2005: 10-11.

Index to Examples of MLA Works Cited

(continued)

(continued)

(*continued*)

Books

1. **One author**

> Joos, Martin. <u>The Five Clocks</u>. New York: Harcourt, 1962.

2. **Two or three authors**

> Mellerman, Sidney, John Scarcini, and Leslie Karlin. <u>Human Development: An Introduction to Cognitive Growth</u>. New York: Harper, 1981.

3. **More than three authors**
Either list only the first name and add "et al." ("and others") or give all names in the order they appear on the title page.

> Spiller, Robert, et al. <u>Literary History of the United States</u>. New York: Macmillan, 1960.

> (or)

> Spiller, Robert, Harlan Minton, Michael Upta, and Gretchen Kielstra. <u>Literary History of the United States</u>. New York: Macmillan, 1960.

4. **More than one work by the same author**
Use the author's name in the first entry only. From then on, type three hyphens and a period and then begin the next title. Alphabetize by title.

> Newman, Edwin. <u>A Civil Tongue</u>. Indianapolis: Bobbs, 1966.

> ---. <u>Strictly Speaking</u>. New York: Warner, 1974.

5. **Work that names an editor as author**
Use the abbreviation "ed." for one editor or "eds." for more than one editor.

> Kinkead, Joyce A., and Jeanette G. Harris, eds. <u>Writing Centers in Context: Twelve Case Studies</u>. Urbana: NCTE, 1993.

6. **Work with an author and an editor**
Give the editor's name after the title. Before the name or names (if there is more than one editor), put the abbreviation "Ed." (for "Edited by").

> Frankfurter, Felix. <u>The Diaries of Felix Frankfurter</u>. Ed. Thomas Sayres. Boston: Norton, 1975.

7. **Work that names a translator**
   Use the abbreviation "Trans." (for "Translated by").

   > Sastre, Alfonso. <u>Sad Are the Eyes of William Tell</u>.
   >   Trans. Leonard Pronko. Ed. George Wellwarth.
   >   New York: New York UP, 1970.

8. **Work by a corporate author**

   > United States Capitol Society. <u>We, the People: The
   >   Story of the United States Capitol</u>. Washington:
   >   Natl. Geographic Soc., 1964.

9. **Work by an unknown author**

   > <u>Report of the Commission on Tests</u>. New York:
   >   College Entrance Examination Board, 1970.

10. **Work that has more than one volume**
    For two or more volumes of a work cited in your paper,
    put references to volume and page numbers in the
    parenthetical references. If you are citing only one of
    the volumes in your paper, state the number of that
    volume in the Works Cited list and give publication
    information for that volume alone.

    > Rutherford, Ernest. <u>The Collected Papers</u>. 3 vols.
    >   Philadelphia: Allen, 1962-65.

    > Stowe, Harriet Beecher. "Sojourner Truth, the
    >   Libyan Sibyl." 1863. <u>The Heath Anthology
    >   of American Literature</u>. Ed. Paul Lauter et
    >   al. 2nd ed. Vol. 1. Lexington: Heath, 1994.
    >   2425-33.

11. **Work in an anthology**
    State the author and title of the work first, then the
    title and other information about the anthology,
    including page numbers on which the selection
    appears.

    > Dymvok, George E., Jr. "Vengeance." <u>Poetry in the
    >   Modern Age</u>. Ed. Jason Metier. San Francisco:
    >   New Horizons, 1994. 54.

    > Licouktis, Michelle. "From Slavery to Freedom." <u>New
    >   South Quarterly</u> 29 (1962): 87-98. Rpt. in
    >   <u>Voices of the Sixties: Selected Essays</u>. Ed.
    >   Myrabelle McConn. Atlanta: Horizons, 1995.
    >   12-19.

12. **Two or more works in the same anthology**
Include a complete entry for the collection and then
cross-reference the works to that collection. In the cross-
reference include the author and title of the work, the
last name of the editor of the collection, and the
inclusive page numbers.

> Batu, Marda, and Hillary Matthews, eds. <u>Voices of
> American Women</u>. New York: Littlefield, 1995.

> Jamba, Shawleen. "My Mother's Not Going Home."
> Batu and Matthews 423-41.

> Little River, Lillian. "Listening to the World." Batu
> and Matthews 234-45.

13. **Article in a reference book**
If the article is signed, give the author first. If it is
unsigned, give the title first. If articles are arranged
alphabetically, omit volume and page numbers. When
citing familiar reference books, list only the edition and
year of publication.

> "Bioluminescence." <u>The Concise Columbia
> Encyclopedia</u>. 2nd ed. 1983.

14. **Introduction, foreword, preface, or afterword**
Start the entry with the author of the introductory part.

> Bruner, Jerome. Introduction. <u>Thought and
> Language</u>. By Lev Vygotsky. Cambridge: MIT P,
> 1962. v-xiii.

15. **The Bible or other sacred text**

> <u>The Jewish Study Bible: Tanakh Translations. Torah,
> Nevi'im, Kethuvim</u>. Trans. Jewish Publication
> Society. Ed. Adele Berlin, Marc Zvi Brettle, and
> Michael Fishbane. Oxford: Oxford UP, 2003.

16. **Work with a title within a title**
If a title normally underlined appears within another title,
do not underline it or put it inside of quotation marks.

> Lillo, Alphonso. <u>Re-Reading Shakespeare's</u> Hamlet
> <u>from the Outside</u>. Boston: Martinson, 1995.

17. **Second or later edition**

> Ornstein, Robert E. <u>The Psychology of Consciousness</u>.
> 2nd ed. New York: Harcourt, 1977.

18. **Modern reprint**
    After the title of the book, state the original publication date. In the publication information that follows, put the date of publication for the reprint.

    > Weston, Jessie L. <u>From Ritual to Romance</u>. 1920. Garden City: Anchor-Doubleday, 1957.

19. **Work in a series**
    If the title page or preceding page of the book indicates it is part of a series, include the series name, without underlines or quotation marks, and the series number, followed by a period, before the publication information.

    > Waldheim, Isaac. <u>Revisiting the Bill of Rights</u>. Studies of Amer. Constitutional Hist. 18. New York: Waterman, 1991.

20. **Work with a publisher's imprint**
    For books under imprints or special names that usually appear with the publisher's name on the title page, include the imprint name and then a hyphen and the name of the publisher.

    > Tamataru, Ishiko. <u>Sunlight and Strength</u>. New York: Anchor-Doubleday, 1992.

21. **Government publication**

    > United States. Office of Education. <u>Tutor-Trainer's Resource Handbook</u>. Washington: GPO, 1973.

22. **Proceedings of a conference**
    Treat the published proceedings of a conference as a book and include information about the conference if such information isn't included in the title.

    > Esquino, Luis. <u>Second Language Acquisition in the Classroom</u>. Proc. of the Soc. for Second Language Acquisition Conf., Nov. 1994, U of Texas. Dallas: Midlands, 1995.

Articles in periodicals

23. **Scholarly journal with continuous paging**
    Most scholarly journals have continuous pagination throughout the whole volume for the year. To find a

particular issue on the shelf, you need only the volume and page numbers, not the issue number.

> Delbruch, Max. "Mind from Matter." <u>American Scholar</u> 47 (1978): 339-53.

24. Scholarly journal that pages each issue separately
If each issue of the journal starts with page 1, then include the issue number.

> Barthla, Frederick, and Joseph Murphy. "Alcoholism in Fiction." <u>Kansas Quarterly</u> 17.2 (1981): 77-80.

25. Abstract of an article

> Cavalier, Jamie C. "The Forgotten Question in Information Technology Strategic Planning." <u>Planning for Higher Education</u> 31 (2002): 5-14. <u>Higher Education Abstracts</u> 18 (2002): item 6703.

26. Monthly or bimonthly magazine article

> Lillio, Debra. "New Cures for Migraine Headaches." <u>Health Digest</u> Oct. 1995: 14-18.

27. Weekly or biweekly magazine article
For a magazine published every week or every two weeks, give the complete date beginning with the day and abbreviating the month. Do not give the volume and issue numbers.

> Isaacson, Walter. "Will the Cold War Fade Away?" <u>Time</u> 27 Feb. 1987: 40-45.

28. Newspaper article
Provide the author's name and the title of the article, then the name of the newspaper as it appears on the masthead, omitting any introductory article such as "The." If the city of publication is not included in the name, add the city in square brackets but not underlined after the name: <u>Journal-Courier</u> [Trenton]. If the paper is published nationally, such as <u>Wall Street Journal</u>, do not add the city of publication. Include the edition if given on the masthead.

> Strout, Richard L. "Another Bicentennial." <u>New York Times</u> 10 Nov. 1994, late ed.: A91.

29. **Article that skips pages**

> Hechinger, John. "Getting Into Day Care Is
> Becoming Harder for Today's Dogs." <u>Wall Street</u>
> <u>Journal</u> 25 May 2005: A1+.

30. **Unsigned article**

> "Trading Lives." <u>Newsweek</u> 21 Apr. 1993: 87-89.

31. **Editorial or letter to the editor**
If you are citing an editorial, add the word "Editorial,"
without an underline or quotation marks, after the title
of the editorial.

> "Watching Hillary's Defense Team at Play." Editorial.
> <u>Washington Times</u> 5 Jan. 1996, late ed.: A18.

32. **Review of a work**
Include the reviewer's name and title of the review, if
any, followed by the words "Rev. of" (for "Review of"),
the title of the work being reviewed, a comma, the word
"by," and then the author's name. If the work has no
title and is not signed, begin the entry with "Rev. of"
and in your list of Works Cited alphabetize under the
title of the work being reviewed.

> Kauffmann, Stanley. "Cast of Character." Rev. of
> <u>Nixon</u>, dir. Oliver Stone. <u>New Republic</u> 22 Jan.
> 1996: 26-27.

> Rev. of <u>The Beak of the Finch</u>, by Jonathan Weiner.
> <u>Science Weekly</u> 12 Dec. 1995: 36.

33. **Article in microform collection of articles**

> Gilman, Elias. "New Programs for School Reform."
> <u>Charleston Herald</u> 18 Jan. 1991: 14.
> <u>NewsBank: School Reform</u> 14 (1991): fiche 1,
> grids A7-12.

Electronic sources

CD-ROMs and other portable databases.   Sources in electronic
form that are stored on CD-ROMs, diskettes, and magnetic
tapes and have to be read on computers are portable databases.
State the medium of publication (such as CD-ROM or diskette),
the vendor's name, and the date of electronic publication.

34. Material accessed from a periodically published database on CD-ROM

If no printed source is indicated, include author, title of material (in quotation marks), date of material (if given), title of database (underlined), publication medium, name of vendor, electronic publication date.

> Anstor, Marylee. "Nutrition for Pregnant Women."
> <u>New York Times</u> 12 Apr. 1994, late ed.: C1.
> <u>New York Times Ondisc</u>. CD-ROM. UMI-
> Proquest. Oct. 1994.

35. Publication on CD-ROM

For CD-ROM publications without updates or regular revisions, cite like books, and add the medium of publication.

> Mattmer, Tobias. "Discovering Jane Austen."
> <u>Discovering Authors</u>. CD-ROM. Vers. 1.0.
> Detroit: Gale, 1992.

36. Publication on diskette

Diskette publications are cited like books with an added description of the medium of publication.

> Lehmo, Jarred. <u>Ethnicity in Dance</u>. Diskette.
> Chicago: U of Chicago P, 1995.

37. Work in more than one published medium

Some electronic publications appear as packages of materials in different publication media. For example, a CD-ROM may be packaged with a diskette. Cite such publication packages as you would a CD-ROM product, specifying the media in the package.

> <u>History of Stage Costuming in Europe</u>. CD-ROM,
> videodisc. Philadelphia: Michelson, 1995.

The Internet and online databases.   Both the Internet and online databases are useful resources. Online databases, like the Internet, are accessed electronically, but online databases may not be linked to the Internet. For example, your library may have purchased databases for some of their computers that are not connected to the Internet.

When you cite sources from the Internet and online databases, you have the same goals as you do when citing print sources: to identify your sources and to help your reader find your sources. But citing electronic sources can be confusing because people who develop sites do not universally agree on what information to include on the site. Moreover, Internet sources change more easily than print sources, and many will not contain all the information you need for a citation. But your aim is to be as complete as possible, to include as much of the information as is available. The basic entry for print sources normally has three main divisions (author, title, and publication information), but a citation for an electronic publication may have as many as five divisions (with periods between each division):

Author's name

Follow the recommendations for citing the names of authors of books.

Title of the document

State the full title of a document that is part of an entire Internet site, and enclose it in quotation marks. (To cite the entire Internet site, see entry 38.)

Information about print publication (if there is a print source)

If the document indicates there is a previous or simultaneous print form of the publication, follow the guidelines for print publications for that part of the citation.

Information about electronic publication

Internet sites vary greatly as to the amount of information provided. Typically you will find the title of the site (underlined in your citation), the date of electronic publication or the latest update, and the name of any institution or organization that sponsors the site. If you see an editor's name or a version number, include that information directly following the title of the site.

Access information

Date of access: Print sources include only one date for publication, but citations to electronic works normally include two (or more) dates, the date for the source and the date on which you viewed the site. If you access the site more than once, include the latest date of access because sites change easily. For a work with a print or simultaneous print existence, it may be necessary to include three dates: the date of print publication, the date of the site, and the date you viewed the site.

URL: The most efficient way to find an online site is to use its network address, known as a URL (uniform resource locator). The sixth edition of the *MLA Handbook* recommends including URLs when citing online works, though URLs are often complex and need to be copied carefully. Because URLs change, include as much other information as you can so that readers can find the site if it has a new address. The *MLA Handbook* also recommends that you print out or download sites you are citing because they might disappear completely from the Internet. Include the URL immediately following the date of access, and enclose the URL in angle brackets. If you need to divide the URL between two lines, break only after a slash and don't include a hyphen at the break. Include the access-mode identifier (http, ftp, gopher, telnet, or news). If the URL you need to include is unusually complicated and lengthy and if there is a search page on the site, give the URL of the site's search page.

Examples of entries for documents found on the Internet:

"Chat Room Libel Case Goes Before State High Court." <u>CNN.com</u>. 2003. Cable News Network. 4 Mar. 2003 <http:// www.cnn.com/2003/US/Northeast/03/04/internet. defamation.ap/index.html>.

Gray, Martin. "Machu Picchu, Peru." <u>Places of Peace and Power</u>. 2005. 28 Sept. 2005 <http://www.sacredsites.com/ americas/peru/machu_picchu.html>.

Scheiber, Noam. "TRB: Norm!" <u>The New Republic</u> 30 May 2005: 6. 9 June 2005 <http://www.tnr.com/thisweek. mhtml?i=20050530>.

Because there will be citations requiring additional information, the following list includes most of the possible types of information that may be needed, listed here in the order they are normally arranged.

- **Name** of the author, editor, compiler, or translator, in reversed order, followed by an abbreviation, if needed, such as "ed." or "trans."

- **Title of the work** enclosed in quotation marks. Or the title of a posting to a discussion list or forum (taken from the subject line and enclosed in quotation marks) followed by the description "Online posting" (not enclosed in quotation marks or underlined)

- **Title of the book** (underlined)

- **Name of the editor, compiler, etc.,** if not already included as the first part of the entry, preceded by an abbreviation such as "Ed." or "Trans."

- **Publication information** for any print version of the source

- **Title of the Internet project or site** (such as a database, online periodical, scholarly project, or personal site) underlined; for a professional or personal site with no title, a description such as "Home page" (neither underlined nor in quotation marks)

- **Name of editor,** if available

- **Version number of the source** or, for a journal, volume number, issue number, or other identifying number

- **Date of electronic publication** of the latest update or of the posting

- **Name of the subscription service** and if a library or consortium of libraries is the subscriber, name and geographical location (city, state abbreviation) of the subscriber (see entry 55)

- **List or forum name** for posting to a discussion list or forum

- **Numbers** (total) of pages, paragraphs, or other sections, if numbered

- **Organization or institution name** that sponsors the site (if not cited earlier)

- **Date of access** (when you accessed the source)

- **Electronic address (URL)** in angle brackets: < > If a URL must be divided between two lines, break it only after a slash, and do not add a hyphen at the break

Gathering information from an Internet site. This illustration indicates where to look for information for your Works Cited information:

URL   Title of Internet project   Title of work

Author

Date of last revision   Institution name

Source: <http://www.olemiss.edu/depts/english/ms-writers/dir/faulkner_william/>.

Work Cited

Padgett, John B. "William Faulkner." <u>Mississippi Writers Page</u>. 15 Apr. 2005. English Dept., U of Mississippi. 9 May 2005 <http://www.olemiss.edu/depts/english/ms-writers/dir/faulkner_william/>.

Kinds of Electronic Publications. **Material accessed through an online database or service.** Online databases or services are not bought in stores or carried around. Access to the Internet is free, but some services or online databases charge a fee. Academic databases are usually accessed through a library (see entry 55). Some additional elements that need to be included in the citation are the name of the service or network through which the database is accessed, the place and date of access, and the network address (URL).

Online Internet site. Typically, to cite an entire online scholarly project, information database, journal, or professional site, include the following items. If you can't find some of this information, cite what is available.

a. Title of the site (underlined)
b. Name of the editor of the site (if given)
c. Electronic publication information, including version number (if relevant and if not part of the title), date of electronic publication or of the latest update, and name of any sponsoring institution or organization
d. Date of access and URL

38. **Material accessed through an online database or service**
    For materials available in print, list information on both the print and online versions, including the date the online version was accessed.

    > Parenti, Michael. "What Does It Mean to Love One's Country?" <u>Peace Review</u> Dec. 2003: 1. <u>Academic Search Elite</u>. EBSCO. Indiana U Lib. 17 June 2004 <http://www.epnet.com/>.

39. **Entire Internet site**

    > <u>CompPile</u>. Ed. Rich Haswell. Aug. 2005. Texas A&M U. 9 Oct. 2005. <http://comppile.tamucc.edu/index.html>.

    > <u>Herbalgram.org</u>. 2002. American Botanical Council. 18 Feb. 2003 <http://www.herbalgram.org>.

40. Home page for a course

Begin the entry with the name of the instructor, reversed, followed by a period, and the title of the course (neither underlined nor in quotation marks). Continue with a description such as "Course home page" (neither underlined nor in quotation marks), with dates of the course, the names of the department and institution, the date of access, and the URL.

> Felluga, Dino F. Nineteenth-Century English Literature. Course home page. Aug. 2000-Dec. 2000. Dept. of English, Purdue U. 9 Mar. 2001 <http://web.ics.purdue.edu/~felluga/337.html>.

41. Home page for an academic department

Give the name of the department, a description such as "Dept. home page" (neither underlined nor in quotation marks), the name of the institution, the date of access, and the URL.

> Horticulture and Landscape Architecture. Dept. home page. Purdue U School of Agriculture. 10 Mar. 2005 <http://www.hort.purdue.edu/hort/academics/program.shtml>.

42. Personal home page

Begin with the name of the person who created it, reversed, followed by a period. Continue with the title of the site (underlined) or, if there is no title, with the description "Home page" (neither underlined nor in quotation marks), the date of the last update, if given; the date of access; and the URL.

> Harris, Muriel. <u>Meet Muriel Harris</u>. 18 June 2002. 9 Apr. 2005 <http://owl.english.purdue.edu/lab/staff/HomePages/mickey.html>.

43. Entire online book

For printed books available online, follow the recommendations for citing books (see entries 1-21), modifying them as appropriate to the electronic source. The following items are typically included:

1. Name of the author, editor, compiler, or translator, in reversed order, followed by an abbreviation, if needed, such as "ed." or "trans."
2. Title of the work (underlined)

3. Name of the editor, compiler, or translator of the book, if that's appropriate and not already included as the first part of the entry, with "Ed.," "Comp.," or "Trans." before the name
4. Publication information for the original print version, if that is included (city of publication, name of publisher, year of publication)
5. Electronic publication information:
   a. Title of the Internet site (underlined)
   b. Name of the editor of the site (if given)
   c. Version number
   d. Date of electronic publication
   e. Name of any sponsoring organization
   f. Date of access and URL

> Yonge, Charlotte. <u>Henrietta's Wish: or Domineering: A Tale</u>. 2nd ed. London. 1853. <u>Victorian Women Writers Project</u>. Ed. Perry Willett. 28 Aug. 1997. Indiana U. 9 Aug. 2002. <http://www.indiana.edu/~letrs/vwwp/yonge/henrietta.html>.

44. Part of an online book
Put the title or name of the part between the author's name and the title of the book. If the part is a work like a poem or essay, put quotation marks around the title of the part.

> Eliot, T[homas] S[terns]. "Whispers of Immortality." <u>Poems</u>. New York: Knopf. 1920. <u>Bartleby.com</u> 1996. 9 Oct. 2005 <http://bartleby.com/199/>.

45. Online government publication

> United States. Department of Defense. Air Force, Air University. <u>Development of Military Night Aviation to 1919</u>. By William Edward Fischer, Jr. 1998. U.S. Govt. Online Bookstore. 10 Mar. 2003 <http://bookstore.gpo.gov/>.

46. Online scholarly project

> Smith, Terry Donovan, and Katie Johnson. "Domestic Life in 19th-Century English Drama." <u>The 19th-Century London Stage: An Exploration</u>. Ed. Jack Wolcott and Joan Robertson. 1999. U of Washington School of Drama. 2 Oct. 2001 <http://artsci.washington.edu/drama-phd/19title.html>.

Online periodicals.   Online periodicals include scholarly journals, newspapers, and magazines, and works within such publications include articles, reviews, editorials, and letters to the
editor. Follow the guidelines for citing parts of print periodicals, modifying them as needed for an electronic source.
Include the author's name; the title of the article or other work
(enclosed in quotation marks); the name of the periodical
(underlined); the volume number, issue number, or other identifying number; the date of publication; the number of pages or
other sections, if numbered; the date of access; and the URL. If
you can't find all this information, cite what is available.

47. **Article in a scholarly journal**
    Scholarly journals may be available independently on
    their own sites or as part of databases. If the journal is
    included in a database, cite the name of the database
    (underlined) after the print information, and follow this
    with the date of access and URL.

    > Carmean, Colleen, and Jeremy Haefner. "Next-
    >   Generation Course Management Systems."
    >   <u>Educause Quarterly</u> 26.1 (2003): 10-13.
    >   <u>Educause</u>. 11 Mar. 2003 <http://www.
    >   educause.edu/ir/library/pdf/eqm0311.pdf>.

48. **Short work from an online scholarly project**

    > Halsall, Paul. "Egypt" <u>Internet History Sourcebooks
    >   Project</u>. 29 July 2001. Fordham University. 27
    >   May 2005 <http://www.fordham.edu/
    >   halsall/>.

49. **Article in a newspaper or newswire**

    > Radford, Tim, ed. "Discovery of a New Species Bucks
    >   Extinction Trend." <u>The Guardian</u> 20 May 2005.
    >   23 May 2005 <http://www.guardian.co.uk/
    >   international/story/0,,1488300,00.html>.

50. **Article in a magazine**

    > Svitil, Kathy A. "How to Weave a Dolphin-Friendly
    >   Net." <u>Discover Magazine</u> 4 Mar. 2005. 15 May
    >   2005. <http://www.discover.com/web-
    >   exclusives/dolphin-friendly-net0304/>.

51. **Anonymous article**

    > "Uh, Folks, Your Data Was Swiped." <u>Wired News</u> 23
    >   May 2005. 1 June 2005. <http://www.wired.
    >   com/news/privacy/0,1848,67616,00.html>.

52. **Online abstract**

> Green, John. "Historical Overview and Basic Facts Involved in the Sasquatch or Bigfoot Phenomenon." <u>Journal of Scientific Exploration</u> 18.1.3 (Spring 2004). Abstract. 1 June 2005 <http://www.scientificexploration.org/jse/ abstracts/v18n1a3.php>

53. **Online review**

> Lehmann, Megan. "Apocalypse Wow." Rev. of <u>The Day After Tomorrow</u>, dir. Roland Emmerich. <u>New York Post Online Edition</u> 28 May 2004. 3 June 2004 <http://www.nypost.com/movies/ 21783.htm>.

54. **Letter to the editor**

> Cripps, Camilla. Letter. <u>Lafayette Journal and Courier Online</u> 25 Mar. 2003. 26 Mar. 2003 <http://www.lafayettejc.com/apps/pbcs.dll/ frontpage>.

Work from a library or personal subscription service. Two types of online subscription services are those to which libraries or library systems typically subscribe (such as InfoTrac or Lexis/Nexis) and those to which users personally subscribe (such as America Online). When you document sources from either type, begin the entry as shown in entry 38, with the title of the site, the name of the editor, the electronic publication information, and the date of access and URL.

The format of the entry depends on whether your source was taken from an information database, an online book, an article from a periodical, and so on. When citing material that originally had a print source, begin with the information about the print publication, omitting whatever is not given in the online version. If you can, conclude with a URL or, if that is complicated and very long, with the URL for the site's search page. If there is no URL, finish your citation as described here.

55. **Library subscription service**
    When you cite a source from a service to which a library or library system subscribes, end the citation with the name of the database you used (underlined), if known; the name of the service; the name of the library or library system (with a city, a state abbreviation, or both if useful); and the date of access. If you know the URL of the service's home page, include that, in angle

brackets, immediately after the date of access. If the service provides only the starting page number of an article's original print version (for example, page 18), include the number followed by a hyphen, a space, and a period: "18- ."

> Gelerntner, David. "Replacing the United Nations" <u>Weekly Standard</u> 17 Mar. 2003: 23-29. <u>Current Affairs</u>. LexisNexis. Purdue U Lib., West Lafayette, IN. 14 Mar. 2003 <http://web.lexisnexis.com/universe>.

56. Personal subscription service

If you use a source from a personal subscription service that retrieves material for you when you enter a keyword or similar designation, complete the citation by writing "Keyword" (not underlined or enclosed in quotation marks), with a colon, and the word itself (or words) following the name of the service and date of access. If you follow a series of topic labels, write the word "Path" (neither underlined nor in quotation marks), with a colon, and list the sequence of topics you followed; use semicolons to separate topics.

> "White and Bleiler Win X-Games." <u>Extreme Sports</u>. America Online. 28 Feb. 2003. Keyword: Action sports.

Other electronic sources. To document other electronic sources, follow the guidelines for print and nonprint sources, and modify as needed. Some kinds of sources will need labels, such as "Interview," "Map," or "Online posting," but do not underline or enclose in quotation marks. If there is an archive available, cite it so that your reader can consult that source.

57. Television or radio program

> Sorkin, Aaron. <u>The West Wing</u>. With Martin Sheen. 5 Mar. 2003. National Broadcasting Company. 12 Mar. 2003 <http://www.nbc.com/The_West_Wing/index.html>.

58. Sound recording or clip

> Nussbaum, Felicity, Joanne Braxton, and Susan Stanford Friedman. "Women's Life Writing." <u>What's the Word?</u> 2001. <u>Modern Language Association</u>. 5 Mar. 2003 <http://www.mla.org/>. Path: MLA Radio Show; Browse Shows and Listen; 2001.

59. Film or film clip

Moore, Michael, dir. <u>Bowling for Columbine</u>. 2002. <u>Film Clips & Soundtrack</u>. 12 Mar. 2003 <http://www.bowlingforcolumbine.com/media/clips/index.php>.

60. Painting, sculpture, or photograph

Gauguin, Paul. <u>In the Vanilla Grove, Man and Horse</u>. 1891. Guggenheim Museum, New York. 9 June 2005 <http://www.guggenheimcollection.org/site/artist_works_50_0.html>.

61. Interview

Rice, Condoleezza. Interview. <u>National Public Radio</u>. 12 Mar. 2003. 14 Mar. 2003 <http://www.npr.org/display_pages/features/feature_1189368.html>.

62. Cartoon

Oliphant, Pat. "Oliphant." Cartoon. <u>Washingtonpost.com</u> 11 Mar. 2003. 15 Mar. 2003 <http://www.washingtonpost.com/wp-dyn/opinion/?nav5hpleft1>.

63. Advertisement

The 2003 Demotivators Calendar. Advertisement. 4 Mar. 2005 <http://www.despair.com/>.

64. E-mail

To cite electronic mail, include the name of the writer; the title of the message (if any) from the subject line, enclosed in quotation marks; a description of the message that includes the name of the person receiving it; and the date of the message.

Harris, David. "Madeleine Albright's Statement." E-mail to the author. 5 Dec. 2004.

65. Online posting

Maxon, Don. "Blending ESL and Bilingual Education." Online posting. 5 Jan. 1998. Dave Sperling Presents ESL Discussion Center Forum for Teachers: Bilingual Education. 6 Feb. 1998 <http://www.eslcafe.com/discussion/ds/index.cgi?read52>.

66. **Synchronous communication**
    When you cite a synchronous communication such as a
    MUD or a MOO, give the name of the speaker, a
    description of the event, the date of the event, the forum
    for the communication, the date of access, and the URL.

    > Garlenum, Karl. Online discussion of peer tutoring.
    > 22 Nov. 1998. WRITE-C/MOO. 27 Nov. 1998
    > <telnet://write-c.udel.edu:2341>.

Other sources

67. **Computer software**
    Citations are similar to those for CD-ROM or diskette
    materials.

    > <u>MacProof</u>. Vers. 3.2.1. Diskette. Salt Lake City:
    > Lexpertise, 1987.

68. **Television or radio program**
    Include the episode title (in quotation marks), the
    program title (underlined), the series title (neither
    underlined nor in quotation marks), the name of the
    network, the call letters and city of the local station,
    and the broadcast date. If pertinent, add information
    such as names of performers, director, or narrator.

    > "Tall Tales from the West." <u>American Folklore</u>. Narr.
    > Hugh McKenna. Writ. Carl Tannenberg. PBS.
    > WFYI, Indianapolis. 14 Mar. 1995.

69. **Record, tape cassette, CD, or DVD**
    Depending on which is emphasized, cite the composer,
    conductor, or performer first. Then list the title
    (underlined), the artist, the medium—if not a compact
    disc (neither underlined nor in quotation marks), the
    manufacturer, and the year of issue (if unknown,
    include "n.d." for "no date"). Place a comma between the
    manufacturer and the date, with periods following all
    other items.

    > Marsalis, Wynton. <u>Baroque Music for Trumpets</u>.
    > English Chamber Orch. Cond. Rayond Leppard.
    > CBS Records, 1988.

    > Schiff, Heinrich. <u>Five Cello Concertos</u>. By Antonio
    > Vivaldi. Academy of St. Martin-in-the-Fields.
    > Dir. Iona Brown. Audiocassette. Philips, 1984.

70. **Film or video recording**
    Begin film citations with the title (underlined), and
    include the director, the distributor, and the year of
    release; you may add the names of the writer, performers,
    and producer. Or start the citation with the name of the
    person whose contribution to the work is your focus. Treat
    a videocassette, videodisc, slide program, or filmstrip like
    a film, and give the original release date and the medium
    before the name of the distributor.

    > Richard III. By William Shakespeare. Dir. Ian
    >   McKellen and Richard Loncrain. Perf. Ian
    >   McKellen, Annette Bening, Jim Broadbent, and
    >   Robert Downey, Jr. MGM/UA, 1995.

    > Renoir, Jean, dir. The Rules of the Game [Le Regle
    >   du Jeu]. Perf. Marcel Dalio and Nora Gregor.
    >   1937. Videocassette. Video Images, 1981.

71. **Live performance of a play**
    Include the theater and city where the performance was
    given, separated by a comma and followed by a period,
    and the date of the performance.

    > Inherit the Wind. By Jerome Lawrence and Robert
    >   E. Lee. Dir. John Tillinger. Perf. George C.
    >   Scott and Charles Durning. Royale Theatre,
    >   New York. 23 Jan. 1996.

72. **Musical composition**
    If the composition is known only by number, form, or
    key, do not underline its title or use quotation marks. If
    the score is published, however, cite it like a book and
    capitalize abbreviations such as "no." and "op."

    > Bach, Johann Sebastian. Brandenburg Concertos.

    > Bach, Johann Sebastian. Orchestral Suite no. 1 in C
    >   major.

73. **Work of art**

    > Monet, Claude. Rouen Cathedral. Metropolitan
    >   Museum of Art, New York. Masterpieces of Fifty
    >   Centuries. New York: Dutton, 1970. 316.

74. **Letter or memo**

    > Blumen, Lado. Letter to Lui Han. 14 Oct. 1990. Lado
    >   Blumen Papers. Minneapolis Museum of Art
    >   Lib., Minneapolis.

75. Personal interview

> Kochem, Prof. Alexander. Personal interview. 18 Apr. 2002.

76. Published interview

> Goran, Nadya. "A Poet's Reflections on the End of the Cold War." By Leonid Tuzman. International Literary Times 18 Nov. 1995: 41-44.

77. Radio or television interview

> Netanyahu, Benyamin. Interview with Ted Koppel. Nightline. ABC. WABC, New York. 18 Aug. 1995.

78. Map or chart

Treat a map or chart like a book without an author (see entry 9), but add the descriptive label "Map" or "Chart."

> New York. Map. Chicago: Rand, 1995.

79. Cartoon

> Adams, Scott. "Dilbert." Cartoon. Journal and Courier [Lafayette] 20 Jan. 1996: B7.

80. Advertisement

> Apple Computer. Advertisement. GQ, Dec. 1999: 145-46.

81. Lecture, speech, or address

> Lihandro, Alexandra. "Writing to Learn." Conf. on Coll. Composition and Communication. Palmer House, Chicago. 23 Mar. 1990.

> Trapun, Millicent. Address. Loeb Theater. Indianapolis. 16 Mar. 2001.

82. Pamphlet

> Thirty Foods for Your Health. New York: Consumers Health Soc., 1996.

83. Published dissertation

If the work was published by University Microfilms International (UMI), add the order number as supplementary information.

> Blalock, Mary Jo. Consumer Awareness of Food Additives in Products Offered as Organic. Diss. U Plainfield, 1994. Ann Arbor: UMI, 1995. 10325891.

84. **Abstract of a dissertation**
Begin with the publication information for the original work, and then add the information for the journal that includes the abstract.

> McGuy, Timothy. "Campaign Rhetoric of Conservatives in the 1994 Congressional Elections." Diss. Johns Hopkins U, 1995. <u>DAI</u> 56 (1996): 1402A.

85. **Unpublished dissertation**

> Tibbur, Matthew. "Computer-Mediated Intervention in Early Childhood Stuttering." Diss. Stanford U, 1991.

40d Sample pages

Research papers that follow MLA style generally do not need a title page, but if you are asked to include one, use the format shown here. Included here also are a first page for a paper that does not have a title page and a first page for the Works Cited list.

1. **Title page following MLA style**

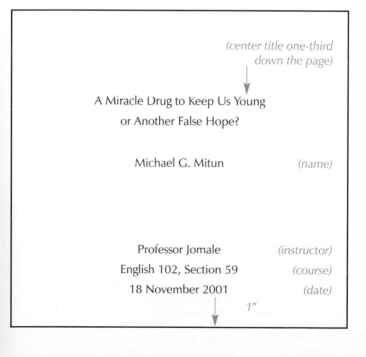

(center title one-third down the page)

A Miracle Drug to Keep Us Young
or Another False Hope?

Michael G. Mitun   *(name)*

Professor Jomale   *(instructor)*
English 102, Section 59   *(course)*
18 November 2001   *(date)*

1"

2. First page following MLA style

1"

Michael G. Mitun

Professor Jomale

English 102

18 November 2001

A Miracle Drug to Keep Us Young

or Another False Hope?

Even before Ponce de Leon landed in Florida in 1513, searching for a fountain of youth, people looked for ways to resist the aging process. Among the unsuccessful cures that we find in history records are ice baths, gold elixirs, and holding one's breath. But now modern medicine is opening the door to new therapies that might work, pills based on hormones that our bodies produce when we're young but that decrease as we grow old. At the moment, the most promising of these hormones is DHEA. But most physicians are unwilling to prescribe DHEA for their patients, and the U.S. Food and Drug Administration has not approved its sale in the United States. At the present time, DHEA shows promise but is not yet the miraculous "fountain of youth" people have been waiting for.

At a recent conference hosted by the New York Academy of Sciences, titled "Dehydroepiandrosterone (DHEA) and Aging," medical researchers reported on their studies of DHEA. Burkhard Bilger, one of the people attending that conference, heard vivid testimonials about this compound which he described as "the most plentiful steroid hormone in the human body—and the most poorly understood" (26). The promise of DHEA suggests that we take a closer look at the evidence to see if medicine really can offer us a new fountain of youth, though the chief of biology Dr. Anna McCormick at the National Institute on Aging warns that there are potential harmful effects (Jaroff).

1"

1"

1"

3. **Works Cited page following MLA style**

Works Cited

Ames, Donna Spahn. "The Effects of Chronic Endurance Training on DHEA and DHEA-S Levels in Middle-Aged Men." Diss. U. of New Hampshire, 1991.

Bilger, Burkhard. "Forever Young." <u>The Sciences</u> Sept./Oct. 1988: 26–30.

Eye to Eye. CBS. WCBS, New York. 15 June 1995.

Fahey, Thomas D. "DHEA." <u>Joe Weider's Muscle and Fitness</u> Aug. 1995: 94–97.

Garcia, Homer. "Effects of Dehydroepiandrosterone (DHEA) on Brain Tissue." <u>DHEA Transformations in Target Tissue</u>. Ed. Milan Zucheffa. London: Binn, 1994: 36–45.

---"Estrogens in Target Tissues." <u>Endocrinology</u> (136 (1997): 3247–56.

<u>Health and Aging</u>. Prod. Hormone Therapy Project, Middleton Medical School. Videodisc. Middleton, 1997.

Jaroff, Leon. "New Age Therapy." <u>Time</u> 23 Jan. 1996: 52.

Li, Min Zhen, ed. <u>The Biologic Role of Dehydroepiandrosterone (DHEA)</u>. Berlin: de Gruyter, 1990.

Mindell, Earl L. "Stay Healthy." <u>Let's Live</u> Sept. 2000. 0–14.

"Nature's Other Time Stopper." <u>Newsweek</u> 7 Aug. 1995: 49.

Oppenheim, Edgar. "DHEA Offers Promise." <u>Springfield Courier</u> 22 June 1995, late ed.: B1. <u>Current News Ondisc</u>. CD-ROM. New York: Qube, 1995.

Rabin, Prof. Jonathan. Personal interview. 21 Oct. 2001.

Rosch, Paul J. "DHEA, Electrical Stimulation, and the Fountain of Youth." <u>Stress Medicine</u> 11.4 (1995): 211–27.

Whaum, Ken. "Re: DHEA testimonials." Online posting. 23 Oct. 1998. Newsgroup alt. health.aging.natural. 2 Nov. 1998 <http://www.dhea.com/discussion/dheabenefits.html>

1"

41

APA Style

American Psychological Association (APA) format is used to document papers in the behavioral and social sciences. If you are asked to use APA format, consult *The Publication Manual of the American Psychological Association*, 5th ed. (Washington, DC: APA, 2001) or their pocket manual, *Concise Rules of APA Style* (Washington, DC: APA, 2005). For updates and additions, see the APA Web site: www.apastyle.org.

APA/MLA similarities

- Both have parenthetical references in the paper to refer readers to the list of sources at the end of the paper.
- Both have numbered notes to include information that would disrupt the main text if included there.
- Both have a reference list of works cited at the end of the paper.
- For both, references include only the sources used in the research and preparation of the paper.

APA/MLA differences

- In APA, the date of publication is included in parenthetical references in the paper and appears after the author's name in the References list at the end of the paper.
- In APA, authors' first and middle names are indicated by initials only.
- In APA, capitalization and use of quotation marks and underlines are different. (See the box below.)
- In APA, put signal words (see 38d) in past tense ("Smith reported") or present perfect tense ("as Smith has reported").

Important Features of APA Style

- For in-text citations, give the author's last name and publication year of the source.
- Use full last names and initials of first and middle names of authors.

(continued)

- Capitalize only the first word and proper names in book and article titles, but capitalize all major words in journal titles. Use italics for titles of books and journals; do not put article titles in quotation marks.
- In the References list, give full publication information, alphabetized by author.

41a In-text citations

Include the author's name and date of publication. For direct quotations, include the page number also.

Examples of APA In-text Citations

1. **Direct quotations**
   When you quote a source, end with quotation marks and give the author, year, and page number in parentheses.

   > Many others agree with the assessment that "this is a seriously flawed study" (Methasa, 1994, p. 22) and do not include its data in their own work.

2. **Author's name given in the text**
   Cite only the year of publication in parentheses. If the year also appears in the sentence, do not repeat by adding parenthetical information. If you refer to the same study again in the paragraph, with the source's name, you do not have to cite the year again if it is clear that the same study is being referred to.

   > When Millard (1970) compared reaction times among the participants, he noticed an increase in errors.

   > In 1994 Pradha found improvement in short-term memory with accompanying practice.

3. **Author's name not given in the text**
   Cite the name and year, separated by a comma.

   > In a recent study of reaction times (Millard, 1970) no change was noticed.

4. **Two or more works by the same author**
   If the author is not named in the text, include the author's name in parentheses and a shortened version of the title of the work cited if both were published in the same year. If the publication dates are different, cite the name and year in each set of parentheses.

   > Recent work on black holes and baby universes indicates the slow progress science made toward understanding these phenomena (Hawking, 1993), and even Albert Einstein, "who was human and fallible" (Hawking, 2001, p. 2001), made mistakes that delayed progress.

5. **Work by two authors**
   For two authors, cite both names every time you refer to the source. Use "and" in the text, but an ampersand (&) in parenthetical material, tables, captions, and the References list.

When Glick and Metah (1991) reported on their findings, they were unaware of a similar study (Grimm & Tolman, 1991) with contradictory data.

6. **Work by three, four, or five authors**
   For three, four, or five authors, include their names (and the year) the first time you cite the source. For additional references, include only the first author's name and "et al." (for "and others"), with no underline or italics.

   Ellison, Mayer, Brunerd, and Keif (1987) studied supervisors who were given no training. Later, when Ellison et al. (1987) continued to study these same supervisors, they added a one-week training program.

7. **Work by six or more authors**
   For six or more authors, cite only the first author's name and "et al." and the year for all references.

   Mokach et al. (1989) noted no improvement in norms for participant scores.

8. **Group as author**
   The name of the group that serves as the author (for example, a government agency or a corporation) is usually spelled out every time it appears in a citation. If the name is long but easily identified by its abbreviation and you want to switch to the abbreviation, give the abbreviation in parentheses when the entire name first appears.

   In 1992 when the National Institute of Mental Health (NIMH) prepared its report, no field data on this epidemic were available. However, NIMH agreed that future reports would correct this.

9. **Work with unknown author**
   When a work has no author, cite the first few words of the reference list entry and the year.

   One newspaper article ("When South Americans," 1987) indicated the rapid growth of this phenomenon.

10. **Authors with the same last name**
    If two or more authors in your References list have the same last name, include their initials in all text citations.

    Until T. A. Wilman (1994) studied the initial survey (M. R. Wilman, 1993), no reports were issued.

11. **Two or more works in the same parentheses**
    When two or more works are cited within the same
    parentheses, arrange them in the order they appear in
    the References list, and separate them with
    semicolons.

    > Several studies (Canin, 1989; Duniere, 1987;
    > Pferman & Chu, 1991) reported similar behavior
    > patterns in such cases.

12. **Work in an anthology**
    Cite the author, year, and, if needed, the page number
    of the work, and indicate in the References that it is
    found in an edited collection.

    > Zarek's (2003) interest in mainstreaming blind
    > students in public schools began when his own
    > daughter was born blind.

13. **Complete work**
    Cite the author of the complete work just as you would
    for one or more authors.

    > With the guidelines for nursing education changing
    > so rapidly, books such as Minhart's (2005) should be
    > required reading for nursing educators.

14. **Multivolume work**
    If not mentioned in the text, indicate the volume you
    are citing.

    > When generic drugs are introduced for general use,
    > they include the warnings, side effects, and
    > instructions for use included with the brand-named
    > versions (Noleither, 3, 2003).

15. **Classical works**
    Reference entries are not necessary for major classical
    works such as ancient Greek and Roman works and the
    Bible, but identify the version you used in the first
    citation in your text. If appropriate, in each citation,
    include the part (book, chapter, lines).

    > This was known (Aristotle, trans. 1931) to be
    > prevalent among young men with these symptoms.

16. **Bible and other sacred texts**
    The first time you use the work, identify the version
    used along with the book, chapter, and lines being

cited. After that, include only the book, chapter, and line numbers.

> Matt chose his theme for the speech after reading 2 Cor. 9:6-10.

17. **Specific parts of a print or electronic source**
   To cite a specific part of a source, include the page, chapter, figure, or table number, and use the abbreviation "p." (for "page") and "chap." (for "chapter").

   > No work was done on interaction of long-term memory and computer programming (Sitwa & Shiu, 1993, p. 224), but recent research (Takamuru, 1996, chap. 6) has considered this interaction.

   For an electronic source that contains no page number, cite the paragraph number with the paragraph symbol (¶) or abbreviation for paragraph (para.). When no paragraph number is given, cite the heading and then number of the paragraph. The Web site for the American Psychological Association (http://www.apastyle.org) has listed an update on how to cite information found on the World Wide Web.

   > The two methods showed a significant difference (Smith, 2000, ¶ 2) when repeated with a different age group.

   > No further study indicated any change in the results (Thomasus, 2001, Conclusion section, para. 3).

18. **Indirect source**
   To cite a source you found in another source (a secondary source), indicate the source you're using, then "as cited in" for the document in which you read it, and include the source you saw that material in. But in your References, cite only the source you used. For example, if you cited work by Author A that you found in the work of Author B, cite only Author B in your References.

   > The most recent work on socializing inmates before they are released from prison indicates that helping them learn a skill has proven to be very effective in keeping them out of prison in the future (Jurano, 2005, as cited in Huang, 2005).

Source in reference

19. **Personal communication**

    Personal communications include letters, memos, some electronic communications (e.g., e-mail, discussion groups, messages on electronic bulletin boards), telephone conversations, and other similar communications. Because the data cannot be recovered, these are included only in the text and not in the References list. Include the initials and last name of the communicator and as exact a date as possible. (For electronic sources that can be documented, see 41c.)

    According to I. M. Boza (personal communication, June 18, 2001), no population studies of the problem were done before 1999.

41b   Footnotes

Content footnotes add important information that cannot be integrated into the text, but they are distracting and should be used only if they strengthen the discussion. Copyright permission footnotes acknowledge the source of quotations that are copyrighted. Number the footnotes consecutively with superscript arabic numerals and include the footnotes on a separate page after the References list. Indent the first line of each footnote.

41c   References list

Arrange entries in alphabetical order by the author's last name, and for several works by one author, arrange by year of publication with the earliest one first. For authors' names, give all surnames first and then the initials. Use commas to separate a list of two or more names, and use an ampersand (&) before the last name in the list. Capitalize only the first word of the title and the subtitle (and any proper names) of a book or article, but capitalize the name of the journal. Italicize book titles, names of journals, and the volume number of the journal.

Start the References list on a new page, with the heading "References" centered at the top of the page (neither underlined nor in quotation marks), and double-space all entries. For each entry in the list, the first line begins at the left margin and all following lines are indented five spaces.

Examples of APA References

(*continued*)

(*continued*)

Books

1. **One author**

   > Rico, G. L. (1983). *Writing the natural way*. Los
   > Angeles: J. P. Tarcher.

2. **Two or more works by the same author**
   Include the author's name in all references and arrange
   by year of publication, the earliest first.

   > Kilmonto, R. J. (1983). *Culture and ethnicity*.
   > Washington, DC: American Psychiatric Press.

   > Kilmonto, R. J. (1989). Comparisons of cultural
   > adaptations. *Modern Cultural Studies, 27*, 237-
   > 243.

3. **Two or more works by the same author in the same year**
   For references by the same author published in the
   same year, alphabetize by the title after the year.
   However, if the references are identified as articles in a
   series, order the references in the series order, not by
   title. Use lowercase letters (a, b, c, etc.) at the end of the
   year, inside the parentheses.

   > Sirohi, K. (2001a). *Forensics casebook: Medicine*.
   > Boston: Ballard.

   > Sirohi, K. (2001b). *Forensics casebook: Anatomy*.
   > Boston: Ballard.

4. **Republication**

   > Dewey, J. (1997). *Experience and education*.
   > Washington, DC: Free Press. (Original work
   > published 1938)

5. **Two or more authors**

   With two or more authors, use the ampersand (&) before the last author. Only list up to and including six authors. If there are seven or more, indicate these by adding "et al."

   > Newhouse, R. A., Stephenson, G. B., Montanegro, A. A., Prenta, C. R., Nehmann, G. T., Zilner, B. L., et al. (1975). *Notes on evolving images.* London: Haymarket.

   > Strunk, W., Jr., & White, E. B. (1979). *The elements of style* (3rd ed.). New York: Macmillan.

6. **Group or corporate author**

   Spell out the full name of the group or corporation. If the publication is a brochure, list this in brackets. When the author is also the publisher, use the word "Author" as the publisher's name.

   > Mental Health Technical Training Support Center. (1994). *Guidelines for mental health nonprofit agency staffs* (2nd ed.) [Brochure]. Manhattan, KS: Author.

7. **Unknown author**

   > *Americana collegiate dictionary* (4th ed.). (1995). Indianapolis, IN: Huntsfield.

8. **Edited volume**

   > Griffith, J. W., & Frey, C. H. (Eds.). (1996). *Classics of children's literature* (4th ed.). Upper Saddle River, NJ: Prentice Hall.

9. **Translation**

   > Lefranc, J. R. (1976). *A treatise on probability* (R. W. Mateau & D. Trilling, Trans.). New York: Macmillan. (Original work published 1952)

10. **Article or chapter in an edited book**

    > Riesen, A. H. (1991). Sensory deprivation. In E. Stellar & J. M. Sprague (Eds.), *Progress in physiological psychology* (pp. 24-54). New York: Academic Press.

11. **Article in a reference book**

> Terusami, H. T. (1993). Relativity. In *The new handbook of science* (Vol. 12, pp. 247-249). Chicago: Modern Science Encyclopedia.

12. **Selection from a foreword, preface, introduction, or afterword**

> Roosevelt, E. (1993). Introduction. In A. Frank. *Diary of a young girl* (B. M. Mooyaart-Doubleday, Trans.) (pp. xiii-xvi). New York: Bantam Books.

13. **Revised edition**

> Telphafi, J. (1989). *Diagnostic techniques* (Rev. ed.). Newbury Park: CA: Pine.

14. **Multivolume work**

> Donovan, W. (Ed.). (1979-1986). *Social sciences: A history* (Vols. 1-5). New York: Hollins.

15. **Technical and research report**

> Birney, A. F., & Hall, M. M. (1981). *Early identification of children with written language disabilities* (Report No. 81-502). Washington, DC: National Education Association.

16. **Report from a university**

> Lundersen, P. S., McIver, R. L., & Yepperman, B. B. *Sexual harassment policies and the law* (Tech. Rep. No. 9). Springfield: University of Central Indiana, Faculty Affairs Research Center.

17. **Classical work**
Reference entries are not required. Instead, identify the version you are using in the first citation in the text.

18. **Bible and other sacred texts**
Reference entries are not required. Instead, identify the version you are using in the first citation in the text.

Articles in periodicals

19. **Article in a journal paged continuously**

> Schaubroeck, J., Sime, W. E., & Mayes, B. T. (1991). The nomological validity of the type A personality. *Journal of Applied Psychology, 76*, 143-168.

20. **Article in a journal paged separately by issue**

> Timmo, L. A., & Kikovio, R. (1994). Young children's attempts at deception. *Research in Early Childhood Learning, 53* (2), 49-67.

21. **Article that skips page numbers**

> Hechinger, J. (2005, May 25). Getting into day care is becoming harder for today's dogs. *The Wall Street Journal*, pp. A1, A7.

22. **Article in a magazine**

> Simmons, H. (1995, November 29). Changing our buying habits. *American Consumer, 21*, 29-36.

23. **Article in a newspaper**

> Leftlow, B. S. (1993, December 18). Corporate takeovers confuse stock market predictions. *The Wall Street Journal*, pp. A1, A14.

24. **Unsigned article**

> New study promises age-defying pills. (1995, July 27). *The Washington Post*, p. B21.

25. **Monograph**

> Rotter, P. B., & Stolz, G. (1966). Generalized expectancies of early childhood speech patterns. *Monographs of the Childhood Education Society, 36* (2, Serial No. 181).

26. **Review of a book, film, or video**
    If the review is untitled, use the material in brackets as the title and indicate if the review is of a book, film, or video; the brackets indicate the material is a description of form and content, not a title.

> Carmody, T. P. (1982). A new look at medicine from the social perspective [Review of the book

> *Social contexts of health, illness, and patient care]. Contemporary Psychology, 27,* 208-209.

Electronic sources

Electronic correspondence (such as e-mail, electronic discussion groups, and so on) is cited as personal communication in your text but does not need to be included in your References list.

All references begin with the same information (or as much as possible) that is included for a print source. World Wide Web information is placed at the end of the reference. Use "Retrieved from" and the date of retrieval because the content of documents can be changed or revised and can be removed from the site. If you have to divide the URL so that it starts on one line and continues on to the next line, break the address before a period or after a slash, and never add a hyphen. Do not use underlining or italics for the URL. See section 40c for a guide to collecting information from a Web site. In APA format, that citation would be formatted as follows:

Reference

Padgett, J. B. (2005, April 15). William Faulkner. *Mississippi writers page.* Retrieved May 9, 2005, from University of Mississippi, English Department Web site: http://www.olemiss.edu/depts/ english/ms-writers/dir/faulkner_william/

27. **Journal article**   ~~use for print also~~
    If the article appears online exactly as it appears in the print source, use the following format:

    Majitsu, K. (2001). Necessary intervention in teenage depression [Electronic version]. *Behavior Intervention, 6,* 36-54.

    If you read an article online from a print source, but you think the online version may have been revised, or if you notice the format differs from the print source or page numbers are not indicated, use the following format:

    Klein, D. F. (1997). Control groups in pharmacotherapy and psychotherapy evaluations. *Treatment, 1.* Retrieved February 9, 1998, from http://journals.apa.org/ treatment/vol1/97_a1.html

28. Article in an Internet-only journal

For an article retrieved via file transfer protocol (FTP), use that URL.

> Greenberg, M. T., Domitrovich, C., & Bumbarger, B. (2001). The prevention of mental disorders in school-aged children: Current state of the field. *Prevention & Treatment, 4.* Retrieved July 18, 2001, from ftp://ftp/journals.apa.org/ prevention/volume4/pre0040001a.html

29. Newspaper article

> Berke, R. L. (2001, July 14). Lieberman put Democrats in retreat on military vote. *New York Times.* Retrieved July 18, 2001, from http://www.nytimes.com

30. Chapter or section in an Internet document

> Berwick, D. M. (n.d.). As good as it should get: Making health care better in the new millennium. In *Policy studies, national coalition on health care* (sec. Adding it up). Retrieved August 1, 2001, from http://www.nchc.org/berwick. html#ADDING

31. Stand-alone document, no author identified, no date

> *Associative learning.* (n.d.). Retrieved July 18, 2001, from http://psy.soton.ac.uk/RGdata/ lbarg/Associative%20Learning.htm

32. Entire Web site

Include the name of the Web site in your text and put the URL in parentheses. Do not include this in your References list.

33. Multipage selection from a Web site

> Badran, A. (2004, May 5). *Developing Egyptian speech recognition using JANUS.* Retrieved June 2, 2005, from http://www.Andrew. cmu.edu/user/ahmedb/EgyptianSR.html

34. Abstract

> Dukas, R. (2001). Effects of perceived danger on flower choice by bees. Abstract retrieved September 23,

2005, from http://psych.mcmaster.ca/
dukas/abstracts.htm#hbpred

35. U.S. government report available on the Web

National Institutes of Health. (n.d.). Stem cells:
Scientific progress and future research.
Retrieved July 19, 2001, from http://www.nih.
gov/news/stemcell/scireport.htm

36. Message posted to a newsgroup

Woodgate, J. (2001, July 16). Calif to change their
voltage? [Msg. 1]. Message posted to news://
sci.electronics.design

37. Message posted to an electronic mailing list

Fischer, K. (2000, January 31). RE: writing
assessment, new twist? Message posted to
WCenter electronic mailing list, archived at
http://www.ttu.edu/wcenter/0002/
msg00014.html

38. E-mail   ~~In text, no reference~~

Personal e-mail and other electronic communications
that are not archived are listed as a personal
communication in the paper and are not listed in the
References list.

39. Electronic database

Center for Public Policy Study. (1994). *Survey of
public response to terrorism abroad: 1992-93.*
Retrieved October 20, 2000, from USGOV
database.

40. CD-ROM

Culrose, P., Trimmer, N., & Debruikker, K. (1996).
Gender differentiation in fear responses [CD-
ROM]. *Emotion and Behavior, 27*, 914-937.
Abstract retrieved July 7, 2001, from
FirstSearch database (PsycLIT Item: 900312).

41. Computer program or software

Gangnopahdhav, A. (1994). Data Analyzer for E-mail
Usage [Computer software]. Princeton, NJ:
MasterMinders.

Other sources

42. Information service

Mead, J. V. (1992). *Looking at old photographs: Investigating the teacher tales that novice teachers bring with them* (Report No. NCRTL-RR-92-4). East Lansing, MI: National Center for Research on Teacher Learning. (ERIC Document Reproduction Service No. ED346082)

43. Dissertation abstract

Rosen, P. R. (1994). Learning to cope with family crises through counselor mediation (Doctoral dissertation, Claremont University, 1994). *Dissertation Abstracts International, 53,* Z6812.

44. Government document

United States Bureau of Statistics. (1994). *Population density in the contiguous United States* (No. A1994-2306). Washington, DC: Government Printing Office.

45. Report from a private organization

American Association of Retired Persons (AARP). (2005, May). *Prescription drugs in Nebraska: A survey of experiences and opinions.* Washington, DC: Author.

46. Conference proceedings

Cordulla, F. M., Teitelman, P. J., & Preba, E. E. (1995). Bio-feedback in muscle relaxation. *Proceedings of the National Academy of Biological Sciences, USA, 96,* 1271-1342.

47. Personal interview
Personal interviews are not included in the References list. Instead, use a parenthetical citation in the text.

48. Published interview
List published interviews under the interviewer's name.

Daly, C. C. (1995, July 14). [Interview with Malcolm Forbes]. *International Business Weekly, 37,* 34-35.

49. **Letter to the editor**

> Strader, L. (2004, June 7). What hypocrisy! (Letter to
> the editor). *Forbes, 173* (12), 30.

50. **Film, videotape, performance, or artwork**
   Start with the name and, in parentheses, functions of
   the originators or primary contributors; put the
   medium, such as film, videotape, slides, etc., in brackets
   after the title; give the name and location of the
   distributor, and if the company is not well known,
   include the address.

> Weiss, I. (Producer), & Terris, A. (Director). (1992).
> *Infant babbling and speech production* [Film].
> (Available from Childhood Research
> Foundation, 125 Marchmont Avenue, Suite
> 224, New York, NY 10022)

51. **Audio recording**

> Totonn, R. (1993). When I wander [Recorded by A.
> Lopper, T. Seagrim, & E. Post]. On *Songs of
> our age* [CD]. Wilmington, ME: Folk Heritage
> Records.

52. **Cassette recording**

> Trussler, R. W., Jr. (Speaker). (1989). *Validity of
> mental measurements with young children*
> (Cassette Recording No. 21-47B).
> Washington, DC: American Psychological
> Measurements Society.

53. **Television broadcast, series, and single episode from a
   series**

> Widener, I. [Executive Producer]. (1995, October 21).
> *Window on the world* [Television broadcast].
> New York: Public Policy Broadcasting.

> Biaccio, R. (Producer). (1994). *The mind of man*
> [Television series]. New York: WNET.

> Nostanci, L. (Writer), & Mindlin, R. (Director).
> (1994). The human sense of curiosity
> [Television series episode]. In R. Biaccio
> (Producer), *The mind of man.* New York:
> WNET.

54. Unpublished paper presented at a meeting

> Lillestein, M. A. (1994, January). *Notes on interracial conflict in college settings.* Paper presented at the meeting of the American Cultural Studies Society, San Antonio, TX.

41d Sample pages

If you are using APA style and asked to include a title page, follow the format shown here for a title page. Included here also are a first page and a first page for the References list.

1. Title page following APA style

(abbreviated title)   ↕ *1/2"*

Militia Organizations   1

(page numbering begins on first page)

(center and double-space)   Militia Organizations: *(title)*

Their Attractions and Appeal

Leila Koach   *(name)*

Prof. McIver   *(instructor)*

Humanities 204   *(course)*

March 22, 2002   *(date)*

---

2. First page following APA style

1/2"

1"

Militia Organizations   2

Militia Organizations: Their Attractions and Appeal

As the number of militia organizations continues to increase (Billman, R. T. 1995), their members are being studied to learn more about the attraction of such groups. A number of factors have surfaced in such interviews. R. Rudner (1994) finds that the publicity surrounding such groups gives meaning to the lives of the members. Other studies (Lattner, 1994; Tobias & Klein, 1994) focus on the feelings of frustration expressed by militia members who typically work in jobs that keep them in lower socio-economic groups. The research project completed by R. Mintz and A. H. Prumanyhuma (1995) indicates that a major attraction of militia groups is their ability to provide members with a strong sense of belonging. These people, who often express accompanying feelings of alienation from society, typically have trouble fitting in elsewhere, a trait noted in several studies (Mukiyama, 1993; Tobias & Klein, 1994). P. Jukan's study (1995) reveals another dimension to the appeal of militias, their announced interest in "getting the government off their backs" (p. 121). A discussion of the results of these studies will provide a profile of typical militia members and their motivations for joining these organizations.

When members profess allegiance to the goals of organizations, they are also giving significance to lives that may otherwise have little meaning. However, as Bryan Liftner, the chair of a recent government task force on terrorism, notes, "allegiance to a group that moves outside of the law or that tries to operate at the thin edges of legality usually reveals a deep sense of allegiance to group goals that, in turn, define the member" (1994, p. 21). This group allegiance is strengthened when militia groups operate in remote areas, thereby placing themselves even farther

1"   1"

1"

3. References page following APA style

References

Billman, R. T., (1995, April 14). Paramilitary groups on the increase. *American Public Policy, 21,* 47–53.

Calimanov, K., Messer, P. B. & Nocatio, L. (1993). *Public Response to Terrorism: 1992–93.* [Electronic database]. (1994). Washington, D.C.: Center for Public Policy Study [Producer and Distributor].

Defense responses of paramilitary groups. (1991). (Report No. 27). Washington, DC: National Crime Prevention Research Project.

Farmer, P. L., Melson, W. W., & Audati, C. J. (1998). Threatening behaviors exhibited by unemployed vs. underemployed individuals. *Current Studies in Psycho-social Behavior, 2.* Retrieved November 12, 1998 from http://www.apa.org/studies/vol2/98_a2.html.

Gumper, M., & Stark, P. T. (1993). *The warrior in postwar culture.* New York: Mayfair.

Jukan, P. (1995). Factors contributing to anti-government organizations' threats of violence. *Journal of Culture and Contemporary Society, 23,* 78–103.

Liftner, B. (1994). *Report on terrorism and weapon use: 1992–1993.* (U. S. Senate Task Force on Terrorism Publication No. 7). Washington, D.C.: Government Printing Office.

Mintz, R., & Prumanyhuma, A. H. (1995). *Social alienation in members of paramilitary groups* (Commission on violence in America Rep. No. 45). Washington, D.C.: U.S. Government Printing Office.

R. Rudner, R. (1994). *Paramilitary doctrines and personal goals, beliefs, and fears.* (Rep. No. 19). New York: City University of New York, Center for the Study of Social Action.

Tamar, R., Sylman, A., Bentur, W., & Foturin, L. (1992). *Paramilitary cultures in post-Vietnam America.* New York: Hampton.

Tobias, C. & Klein, J. T. (1994). Socioeconomic factors in feelings of alienation. *American Journal of Psychiatric Studies, 33,* 256–73.

42

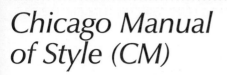

Chicago Manual of Style (CM)

In disciplines such as history and other fields of study in the humanities, the preferred style is *Chicago Manual (CM)*. The most recent guide for this format is *The Chicago Manual of Style*, 15th ed. (Chicago: U of Chicago P, 2003). A shorter volume on Chicago style, for student writers, is the following:

> Turabian, Kate L. *A Manual for Writers of Term Papers, Theses, and Dissertations*. 6th ed. Rev. John Grossman and Alice Bennett. Chicago: U of Chicago P, 1996.

When you use *Chicago Manual* style, include (1) notes (or endnotes) to cite references in the text and (2) a bibliography at the end of the paper to list those works referred to in the notes.

Notes in Chicago Style:

Numbering in the Text

- Number citations consecutively with superscript numbers ([1]) for publication information or for explanations and additional material that would interrupt the main text if inserted there.

- Put the note number at the end of the citation, preferably following the last punctuation mark of the sentence with no space between the mark and the number.

> The violence in the Raj at that time was more pronounced than it had been in the previous conflict.[4] But, as has been noted by Peter Holman, "the military police were at a loss to stem the tide of bloodshed."[5]

Placing Notes

- List notes at the bottom of the page as footnotes or at the end of the essay as endnotes.

Spacing Notes

- Single-space individual notes, with the first line indented three spaces.

- Single-space between notes.

Ordering the Parts of Notes

- Begin with the author's first name and then last name.

- Then add the title(s).

- Then include the publishing information and page numbers.

Punctuating, Capitalizing, and Abbreviating

- Use commas between elements, and put publishing information within parentheses.

- Include the page number, but omit the abbreviation "p" or "pp."

- Underline or italicize titles of books and periodicals.

- Capitalize titles of articles, books, and journals.

- Use quotation marks around parts of books or articles in periodicals.

- Do not abbreviate the name of the publisher.

Later Notes

- The first time you cite a source, include all the relevant information. Shorten later citations for that source.

- For most cases, note the author's last name, followed by a comma; give the main title, shortened if more than four words; and include the page(s) cited, but omit "p." or "pp."

- If you wish, use "ibid." to refer to the work in the previous note or, if the page is different, use "ibid." followed by a comma and the page number.

   6. Peter Holman, *The History of the Raj: Nineteenth and Twentieth Centuries* (New York: Dorset Press, 1996), 18.

   7. George Frederick Abbot, *Israel in Europe* (New York: Humanities Press, 1972), 54.

8. Holman, *History of the Raj*, 34-36.

9. Ibid., 72.

Bibliography in *Chicago* Style

- Differences between the notes and the bibliography:

  - Notes have names in natural order (first name, then last name); the bibliography inverts the first author's name, with last name first.
  - Elements in the bibliography are separated by periods, not commas and parentheses.

  Holman, Peter. *The History of the Raj: Nineteenth and Twentieth Centuries*. New York: Dorset Press, 1996.

- Use the title "Bibliography," but it can also be "Select Bibliography," "Works Cited," or "References."

- Start with the first line at the left margin and indent other lines in the entry three spaces. Single-space throughout.

- Include all the elements that were in the first note for that source but do not put parentheses around the publishing information.

- Underline or italicize titles of books and periodicals.

- Use quotation marks around parts of books or articles in periodicals.

- Do not abbreviate the name of the publisher.

Parts of the bibliography (in the order they appear):

Author:	–full name of author(s), editor(s), and translator(s)
Title:	–full title, including subtitle
Editor, compiler, or translator:	–if any and if in addition to the author
Volumes:	–total number of volumes if referred to as a whole
Volume number:	–if a single volume in the whole work is cited
Title of individual volume:	–if applicable
Facts of publication:	–city, publisher's full name, and date
Page number(s):	–or volume and page number if any

Examples of CM-Style Notes and Bibliogr

(continued)

(N = Note; B = Bibliography)

Books

1. **One author**
   N:　　　1. George Frederick Abbot, *Israel in Europe* (New York: Humanities Press, 1972), 18.
   B:　Abbot, George Frederick. *Israel in Europe.* New York: Humanities Press, 1972.

2. **Two or three authors**
   N:　　　2. A. Y. Yodfat and Y. Arnon-Channa, *P.L.O. Strategy and Tactics* (London: Croom Helm, 1981), 45.
   B:　Yodfat, A. Y., and Y. Arnon-Channa. *P.L.O. Strategy and Tactics.* London: Croom Helm, 1981.

3. **Four or more authors**
   For a work by four to ten authors, give the name of the first author, followed by "and others" (or by "et al.") with

no intervening punctuation, in a note. Give the names
of all the authors in the bibliography.

N: 3. John K. Fairbank and others, *East Asia:
           Tradition and Transformation* (Boston: Houghton
           Mifflin, 1973), 274-75.
B: Fairbank, John K., Edwin O. Reischauer, George
           Allen, and Albert Craig. *East Asia: Tradition
           and Transformation.* Boston: Houghton
           Mifflin, 1973.

For a work by more than ten authors, just list the first
seven, followed by "et al."

4. Unknown author
N: 4. *The Chicago Manual of Style*, 15th ed.
           (Chicago: University of Chicago Press, 2003), 420.
B: *The Chicago Manual of Style.* 15th ed. Chicago:
           University of Chicago Press, 2003.

5. Editor or translator
N: 5. Dan Caspi, Abraham Diskin, and
           Emmanuel Gutmann, eds., *The Roots of Begin's
           Success* (New York: St. Martin's Press, 1984), 36.
B: Caspi, Dan, Abraham Diskin, and Emmanuel
           Gutmann, eds. *The Roots of Begin's Success.*
           New York: St. Martin's Press, 1984.

6. Edition other than the first one
N: 6. John Joseph Mathews, *The Osages:
           Children of the Middle Waters*, 2nd ed. (Norman:
           University of Oklahoma Press, 1963), 145-47.
B: Mathews, John Joseph. *The Osages: Children of
           the Middle Waters.* 2nd ed. Norman:
           University of Oklahoma Press, 1963.

7. Selection or book chapter in an anthology
N: 7. Emmanuel Anati, "The Prehistory of the
           Holy Land (until 3200 BC)," in *A History of the
           Holy Land*, ed. Michael Avi-Yonah (Jerusalem:
           Jerusalem Publishing House, 1969), 33-41.
B: Anati, Emmanuel. "The Prehistory of the Holy Land
           (until 3200 BC)." In *A History of the Holy
           Land*, edited by Michael Avi-Yonah, 33-41.
           Jerusalem: Jerusalem Publishing House, 1969.

8. Multivolume book
N: 8. Cao Xuequin, *The Story of Stone*, trans.
           David Hawkes (Harmondsworth: Penguin Books,
           1977), 2:150-51.

B: Xuequin, Cao. *The Story of Stone.* translated by David Hawkes. Vol. 2. Harmondsworth: Penguin Books, 1977.

9. **Work in a series**
   N: 9. Sean Wilentz, *Major Problems in the Early Republic 1787-1848: Documents and Essays,* Major Problems in American History Series (Lexington: D. C. Heath, 1992), 27-45.
   B: Wilentz, Sean. *Major Problems in the Early Republic 1787-1848: Documents and Essays.* Major Problems in American History Series. Lexington: D. C. Heath, 1992.

10. **Reference book**
    N: 10. *Encyclopaedia Britannica,* 15th ed., s.v. "Henry Clay."

    (Do not include the volume or page number. Instead, cite the term in the reference book under which the information is contained. Use the abbreviation "s.v." for "sub verbo," meaning "under the word.")

    B: Well-known reference books are not usually listed in the bibliography.

11. **Biblical or other scriptural reference**
    N: 11. Gen. 21:14-18.

    (Include the book in roman type, abbreviated with no underline or italics, chapter, and verse. Do not use a page number.)

    B: Scriptural references are usually cited only in the notes.

Periodicals

12. **Article in a journal paginated by volume**
    N: 12. Russell Reid, "Journals of the Atkinson-O'Fallon Expedition," *North Dakota Historical Quarterly* 4 (1929): 5-56.
    B: Reid, Russell. "Journals of the Atkinson-O'Fallon Expedition." *North Dakota Historical Quarterly* 4 (1929): 5-56.

13. **Article in a journal paginated by issue**
    N: 13. Carl Coke Rister, "The Significance of the Destruction of the Buffalo in the Southwest," *Southwestern Historical Society* 33, no. 1 (1929): 44-57.

B: Rister, Carl Coke. "The Significance of the Destruction of the Buffalo in the Southwest." *Southwestern Historical Society* 33, no. 1 (1929): 44-57.

14. Article in a magazine

N: 14. Jacob Schlesinger, "Sundown," *New Republic*, August 3, 1998, 12.

B: Schlesinger, Jacob. "Sundown." *New Republic*, August 3, 1998, 12.

15. Article in a newspaper

Include the section number with "sec." but not the page on which the article appears.

N: 15. Barbara Crossette, "New U.N. Push to Urge Iraq to Cooperate with Inspectors," *New York Times*, August 8, 1998, sec. A.

B: Crossette, Barbara. "New U.N. Push to Urge Iraq to Cooperate with Inspectors." *New York Times*, August 8, 1998, sec. A.

16. Unsigned article

N: 16. "Identifying Alcohol Poisoning," *Town Journal*, June 2, 2005, sec. A.

B: "Identifying Alcohol Poisoning." *Town Journal*, June 2, 2005. sec. A.

17. Book review

N: 17. Bernard Lewis, review of *Autumn of Fury: The Assassination of Anwar Sadat*, by Mohamed Heikal, *New York Review of Books*, May 31, 1984, 25-27.

B: Lewis, Bernard. Review of *Autumn of Fury: The Assassination of Anwar Sadat*, by Mohamed Heikal. *New York Review of Books*, May 31, 1984, 25-27.

(This information can be included instead in the notes or in the text.)

18. Published letter

N: 18. Stephen Targema, letter to the editor, *Wall Street Journal*, January 12, 2004, sec. A.

B: Targema, Stephen. Letter to the editor. *Wall Street Journal*. January 12, 2004, sec. A.

Electronic sources

The *Chicago Manual of Style* does not recommend including the date you access the site unless it is time-sensitive. But you can include an access date after the URL.

19. Information service

N: 19. Linda Flower, "Diagnosis in Revision: The Experts' Option," Communications Design Center Technical Report No. 27 (Pittsburgh: Carnegie Mellon University, 1986), OVID, ERIC ED 266464.

B: Flower, Linda. "Diagnosis in Revision: The Experts' Option." Communications Design Center Technical Report No. 27. Pittsburgh: Carnegie Mellon University, 1986. OVID, ERIC ED 266464.

20. Online database

N: 20. Pennti Aalto, "Swells of the Mongol-Storm around the Baltic." *Acta Orientalia* 36 (Budapest, 1982): 5-15, in *Bibliography of Asian Studies* [database online]; available from OVID Information Services, Inc., Murray, UT, identifier no. 19980218.232.

B: Aalto, Pennti. "Swells of the Mongol-Storm around the Baltic." *Acta Orientalia* 36 (Budapest, 1982): 5-15. In *Bibliography of Asian Studies* [database online]. Murray, UT: OVID Information Services, Inc. Identifier no. 19980218.232.

21. Web site

N: 21. *The Internet Movie Database*, http://imdb.com.

B: *The Internet Movie Database*. http://imdb.com.

22. Document from a Web site

N: 22. Lucia Sommer, "Simon Penny's Electronic Critique: Notes on the Politicization of Art against the Aestheticization of Politics," *Cultronix* 1 (Pittsburgh: Carnegie Mellon University, 1994), http://eserver.org/cultronix/sommer (accessed January 28, 1995).

    B.   Sommer, Lucia. "Simon Penny's Electronic Critique: Notes on the Politicization of Art against the Aestheticization of Politics." *Cultronix* 1. Pittsburgh: Carnegie Mellon University, 1994. http://eserver.org/cultronix/sommer (accessed January 28, 1995).

23. E-mail

E-mail that is personal and not archived on a Web site should be treated as personal communication and not included in the bibliography.

    N: 23. Bekki Kaplan, e-mail message to author, June 15, 2005.

24. Online mailing list

Online mailing lists that have been archived on a Web site should include the URL after the date but are not included in the bibliography.

    N: 24. Victoria Fisher, posting to Educational Technology mailing list, May 31, 2005, http://groups.beta.google.com/group/bit.listserv.edtech/.

25. CD-ROM

    N: 25. *All-Movie Guide*, CD-ROM (Corel, 1996).
    B: *All-Movie Guide*. CD-ROM. Corel, 1996.

26. Computer software

    N: 26. CensusCounts. Ver. 2.1, Decisionmark Corporation, Cedar Rapids, IA.
    B: CensusCounts. Ver. 2.1. Decisionmark Corporation, Cedar Rapids, IA.

Other sources

27. Government publication

    N: 27. William Lilley, *The State Atlas of Political and Cultural Diversity* (Washington, DC: Congressional Quarterly, 1997), 31-45.
    B: Lilley, William. *The State Atlas of Political and Cultural Diversity*. Washington, DC: Congressional Quarterly, 1997.

28. Unpublished dissertation

    N: 28. Arnold Mayniew, "Historical Perceptions of Royal Prerogative" (PhD diss., University of Illinois, 1991), 32-37.

B: Mayniew, Arnold. "Historical Perceptions of Royal
Prerogative." PhD diss., University of
Illinois, 1991.

29. Interview
N: 29. David Gergen, interview by Ted Koppell,
Nightline, American Broadcasting Company,
August 18, 1998.

B: Gergen, David. Interview by Ted Koppell.
Nightline. American Broadcasting Company,
August 18, 1998.

30. Personal communications
N: 30. Maynard Jimmerson, telephone
interview with author, July 27, 2004.

Personal communications are mentioned within the text
or in the notes, but they are not usually included in the
bibliography.

31. Film or videotape
N: 31. *The Luttrell Psalter: Everyday Life in
Medieval England*, VHS, produced and directed
by Martin Shuman. (Princeton, NJ: Films for the
Humanities & Sciences, 1994).

B: *The Luttrell Psalter: Everyday Life in Medieval
England*. VHS. Produced and directed by
Martin Shuman. Princeton, NJ: Films for
the Humanities & Sciences, 1994.

32. Television
N: 32. "Castles and Dungeons," *Modern
Marvels*, The History Channel (New York: A&E
Television Networks), June 9, 2005.

B: "Castles and Dungeons." *Modern Marvels*. The
History Channel. New York: A&E Television
Networks, June 9, 2005.

33. Art
N: 33. Georges-Pierre Seurat. *Evening,
Honfleur* (New York: Museum of Modern Art).

B: Seurat, Georges-Pierre. *Evening, Honfleur*. New
York: Museum of Modern Art.

34. Advertisement
N: 34. Bank of America, advertisement, *Time*,
June 6, 2005.

B: Bank of America. Advertisement. *Time*. June 6,
2005.

35. Sound recording

N: 35. J. S. Bach, *Four Concerti for Various Instruments*, Orchestra of St. Luke's, Michael Feldman, Musical Heritage Society, Inc. 512268T (compact disc).

B: Bach, J. S. *Four Concerti for Various Instruments*. Orchestra of St. Luke's. Michael Feldman. Musical Heritage Society, Inc. 512268T (compact disc).

36. Source quoted from another source

N: 36. H. H. Dubs, "An Ancient Chinese Mystery Cult," *Harvard Theological Review* 35 (1942): 223, quoted in Susan Naquin, *Millenarian Rebellion in China: The Eight Trigrams Uprising of 1813* (New Haven: Yale University Press, 1976), 288.

B: Dubs, H. H. "An Ancient Chinese Mystery Cult." *Harvard Theological Review* 35 (1942): 223. Quoted in Susan Naquin, *Millenarian Rebellion in China: The Eight Trigrams Uprising of 1813*. New Haven: Yale University Press, 1976.

43

Council of Science Editors (CSE)

Writers in the physical and life sciences follow the documentation style developed by the Council of Science Editors (CSE) and found in *Scientific Style and Format: The CBE Manual for Authors, Editors, and Publishers*, 6th ed. (New York: Cambridge UP, 1994). The Council of Science Editors, which had previously been known as the Council of Biology Editors, CBE, is currently preparing a seventh edition of this book. (See their Web site, <http://www.councilscienceeditors.org/publications/style.cfm>.) Until the new edition appears, the CSE relies on

The National Library of Medicine Recommended Formats for Bibliographic Citation with the supplement "Internet Formats" by Karen Patrias. (<http://www.nlm.nih.gov/pubs/formats/internet.pdf>). Mathematicians use either this style or the style in the book listed in section 44, under the entry for "Mathematics." (Section 44 also lists style manuals for other scientific fields.)

The CBE Style Manual offers two documentation styles, and you can ask your instructor which one is preferred for your papers. Or you can check a current journal in the field. The two styles are:

- **Authors' names and publication dates**

  Here, authors' names and publication dates are included in parenthetical citations in the text, closely resembling the APA style (see section 41).

  In-text citation:

  > The earlier studies done on this virus (Fong and Townes 1992; Mindlin 1994) reported similar results. However, one of these studies (Mindlin 1994) noted a mutated strain.

  In the list of references at the end, the names are listed alphabetically with the date after the name.

  Reference list:

  > 1. Fong L, Townes IIC. (1992). Viral longevity. Biol Rep 27: 129-45.

- **In-text numbered references**

  In this format, references are listed with in-text superscript numbers (numbers set above the line, such as [1] and [2]) that refer to a list of numbered references at the end. The references are numbered according to the order in which they are used in the text, and later references to the same work use the original number. When you have two or more sources cited at once, put the numbers in sequence and separate them with commas but no spaces.

  In-text citation:

  > The earlier studies done on this virus[1,4,9] reported similar results. However, one of these studies[4] noted a mutated strain.

In the list of references at the end, list the entries in numerical order, according to the order in which they are cited in the paper, not alphabetically.

Reference list:

> 1. Fong L, Townes H. Viral longevity. Biolog Rep 1992;27:129-45.

CSE Reference List

At the end of the paper, include a list entitled "References" (or "Cited References"). The placement of the date within the entries will differ, depending on which format you use.

Name and publication date format

- Put the date after the author's name.

- Arrange the list alphabetically by last names.

- Do not indent any lines in the entries.

In-text numbered references

- Put the date after the publisher's name for books.

- Put the date after the periodical name for references to periodicals.

- Arrange the list by number.

- Put the number at the left margin, followed by the authors' last names. For the second and following lines, align beneath the first letter of the line above.

> 1. xxxxxxxxxxxxxxxxxxx
>   xxxxxxxxxx
> 2. xxxxxxxxxxxxxxxxxxx
>   xxxx

Parts of the reference:

(Use periods between major divisions of the entry):

Author's name	–Start with last name first, no comma, and initials without periods for first and middle names. Separate authors' names with commas. End the list of authors' names with a period.
Title	–For books and article titles, use capitals only for the first word and proper nouns. Do not use under-

line, italics, or quotation marks. For journals, abbreviate titles and capitalize all major words.

Place of publication (colon), publisher (semicolon), and publication date (period)	—Include a space between the full name of the publisher and the date. Use a semicolon with no space between the date and the volume number of the journal. Abbreviate months but do not use a period.
Number of pages	—For books, include the total number of pages in the book, with a space and then a "p" after the number. End the entry with a period. For journal articles, show the total number of pages of the article, and for the second number use only numbers not already included in the first number (for example: 122–7; 49–51; 131–8; 200–9). End with a period.

Examples of CSE Format for Reference List

1. **Books with one author**

   Glenn EP. Encyclopedia of environmental biology. San Diego: Academic Press; 1995. 1289 p.

2. **Books with more than one author**

   Rouse Ball WW, Coxeter HSM. Mathematical recreations and essays. 13th ed. Mineola, NY: Dover Publications; 1987. 381 p.

3. **Books with an editor**

   Estes JW, Smith BG, editors. A melancholy scene of devastation: the public response to the 1793 Philadelphia yellow fever epidemic. Philadelphia: Science History Publications/USA; 1997. 436 p.

4. **Organization as author**

   Council of Science Editors. Scientific style and format: the CSE manual for authors, editors, and publishers. 6th ed. New York: Cambridge UP; 1994. 704 p.

5. **Section of a book**

   Saari JC. Retinoids in photosensitive systems. In: Sporn MB, editor. The retinoids. 2nd ed. New York: Raven Press; 1994. p 351-78.

6. **Article in a scholarly journal**

   Adleman LM. Molecular computation of solutions to combinatorial problems. Science 1994;266: 1021-4.

7. **Newspaper or magazine article**

   Allen A. Mighty mice: the perils of patenting genes. The New Republic 1998 Aug 10;16-8.

8. **Article with no author**

   Begin the entry with "[Anonymous]."

9. **Editorial**

   After the title, add "[editorial]."

10. **Audiovisual materials**
    The CSE Manual does not have guidelines for CD-ROM sources, but the format shown here is a suggested model to follow.

Recent developments in DNA models [videocassette].
Miletius T, editor. DistanceED Productions,
producer. [San Diego]: Media Forum; 1997. 3
videocassettes: 315 min, sound, color, 1/2 in.
(Genetics Laboratories; Nr. 9). Accompanied by: 3
guides. Available from: Boston National Visual
Instruction Library, Boston, MA.

11. **Electronic journal articles**

Arlinghaus SL, Drake WD, Nystuen, JD. Animaps.
Solstice: an electronic journal of geography and
mathematics [serial on the Internet]. 1998 [cited
2001 Apr 9];9(1): [about 3 p.] Available from: http://
www-personal.umich.edu/~sarhaus/image/
animaps.html

12. **Web sources**
The CSE Manual recommends the formats explained in
the *National Library of Medicine Recommended Formats
for Bibliographic Citations*' "Supplement: Internet
Formats" (http://www.councilscienceeditors.
org/publications/style.cfm). To cite a portion of a Web
site, use the format for that type of document
(monograph, serial, or database). For a home page, cite
the following elements in the order shown:

* Author
* Author's affiliation
* Content designator ("Homepage" may be inserted here in brackets)
* Medium designator ("Internet" may be inserted here in brackets)
* Place of publication
* Publisher
* Date of publication or copyright
* Date of update or revision
* Date of citation
* Availability (the URL preceded by the phrase "Available from")

Surguladze N, Patton S, Cozzi A, Fried MG, Connor
JR. (Department of Molecular and Cellular
Biochemistry, University of Kentucky, Lexington, KY),
Characterization of nuclear ferritin and mechanism of
translocation. Gt. Brit. Biochem J [Internet]. 2005
[cited 2005 Jun 15];388:731-40. Available from http://
www.biochemj.org/bj/388/bj3880731.htm

44

Style Manuals for Various Fields

Anthropology

The Chicago Manual of Style (see section 42) and *Webster's 10th New Collegiate Dictionary* On its Web site, the American Anthropological Association offers a brief "AAA Style Guide": http://www.aaanet.org/pubs/style_guide.htm

Astronomy

See entry for Physics.

Biology

Council of Science Editors. *Scientific Style and Format: The CBE Manual for Authors, Editors, and Publishers.* 6th ed. New York: Cambridge UP, 1994: http://www.councilscienceeditors.org/publications/style.cfm

Business

American Management Association. *The AMA Style Guide for Business Writing.* New York: AMACOM, 1996.

Chemistry

Dodd, Janet S., ed. *The ACS Style Guide: A Manual for Authors and Editors.* 2nd ed. Washington: Amer. Chemical Soc., 1997.

Earth Sciences

Bates, Robert L., ed. *Geowriting: A Guide to Writing, Editing, and Printing in Earth Science.* 5th ed. Alexandra: Amer. Geological Inst. 1995.

Education

APA (see section 41) and MLA (see section 40).

English

Gibaldi, Joseph. *MLA Handbook for Writers of Research Papers.* 6th ed. New York: MLA, 2003. (See section 40.)

Government

United States Government Printing Office. *Style Manual.* Washington: GPO, 2000.

Health Sciences

Atlas, Michel C. *Author's Handbook of Styles for Life Science Journals.* Boca Raton: CRC Press, 1996.

O'Connor, Andrea B. *Writing for Nursing Publications.* Thorofare, NJ: Slack, 1988.

History

The Chicago Manual of Style (see section 42).

Journalism

Connolly, William, and Allan Siegal. *New York Times Manual of Style and Usage.* New York: Times Books, 1999.

Goldstein, Norm, et al. *Associated Press Style Book and Briefing on Media Law.* Rev. and updated ed. Portland: Perseus Press, 2002.

Law

Harvard Law Review Staff. *The Bluebook: A Uniform System of Citation.* 18th ed. Cambridge: Harvard Law Review Assoc., 2005.

Library Science

Garner, Diana, Diane H. Smith, and Gapner, Diane. *Complete Guide to Citing Government Information Resources: A Manual for Writers and Librarians.* Rev. ed. Bethesda: Congressional Information Services, 1993.

Mathematics

American Mathematical Society. *The AMS Author Handbook: General Instructions for Preparing Manuscripts.* Providence: AMS, 1996.

Medicine

Iverson, Cheryl, et al. *American Medical Association Manual of Style.* 9th ed. Baltimore: Williams and Wilkins, 1998.

Music

Holoman, D. Kern, Ed. *Writing about Music: A Style Sheet from the Editors of* 19th-Century Music. Berkeley: U of California P, 1988.

Philosophy

Guidebook for Publishing in Philosophy. Newark, DE: American Philosophy Assoc., 1997.

Physics and Astronomy

American Institute of Physics. *AIP Style Manual.* 4th ed. College Park, MD: AIP, 1990.

Waldron, Anne, Peggy Judd, and Valerie Miller. *Physical Review Style and Notation Guide.* Minor rev. New York: Amer. Physical Soc., 2005. http://authors. aps.org/STYLE/

Political Science

Lane, Michael K. *Style Manual for Political Science.* Rev. ed. Washington: Amer. Political Science Assn., 2002.

Psychology

American Psychological Association. *Publication Manual of the American Psychological Association.* 5th ed. Washington: APA, 2001. (See section 41.)

Science and Technical Writing

Microsoft Corporation. *Microsoft Manual of Style for Technical Publications.* 3rd ed. Redmond: Microsoft, 2003.

Social Work

National Association of Social Workers. *Writing for the NASW Press.* Washington, DC: NASW Press, n.d. http://www.naswpress.org/resources/tools/01-write/guidelines_toc.htm

Sociology

American Sociological Association. *ASA Style Guide.* 2nd ed. Washington, DC: ASA, 1997. http://www. calstatela.edu/library/bi/rsalina/asa.styleguide. html

Johnson, William A., Rettig, Richard P., Scott, Gregory M., Garrison, Stephen M. *The Sociology Student Writer's Manual,* 4th ed. Upper Saddle River: Prentice Hall, 2003.

Glossary of Usage

This list includes words and phrases you may be uncertain about when writing. If you have questions about words not included here, try the index at the back of this book to see whether the word is discussed elsewhere. You can also check a recently published dictionary.

A, An Use *a* before words beginning with a consonant and before words beginning with a vowel that sounds like a consonant:

a cat   a house   a one-way street   a union   a history

Use *an* before words that begin with a vowel and before words with a silent *h*.

an egg   an ice cube   an hour   an honor

Accept, Except *Accept*, a verb, means *to agree to, to believe, or to receive.*

The detective **accepted** his account of the event.

Except, a verb, means *to exclude or leave out*, and *except*, a preposition, means *leaving out*.

Because he did not know the answers, he was **excepted** from the list of contestants and asked to leave.

Except for brussel sprouts, I eat most vegetables.

Advice, Advise *Advice* is a noun, and *advise* is a verb.

She always offers too much **advice**.

Would you **advise** me about choosing the right course?

Affect, Effect Most frequently, *affect*, which means *to influence*, is used as a verb, and *effect*, which means *a result*, is used as a noun.

The weather **affects** my ability to study.

What **effect** does coffee have on your concentration?

However, *effect*, meaning *to cause or bring about*, is also used as a verb.

The new traffic enforcement laws **effected** a change in people's driving habits.

Common phrases with *effect* include the following:

in effect   to that effect

255

Ain't   This is a nonstandard way of saying *am not, is not, has not, have not*, and so on.

All Ready, Already   *All ready* means *prepared*; *already* means *before* or *by this time*.

> The courses for the meal are **all ready** to be served.

> When I got home, she was **already** there.

All Right, Alright   *All right* is two words, not one. *Alright* is an incorrect form.

All Together, Altogether   *All together* means *in a group*, and *altogether* means *entirely, totally*.

> We were **all together** again after having separate vacations.

> He was not **altogether** happy about the outcome of the test.

Alot, A Lot   *Alot* is an incorrect form of *a lot*.

a.m., p.m. (or) A.M., P.M.   Use these with numbers, not as substitutes for the words *morning* or *evening*.

> We meet every ~~a.m.~~ for an exercise class.

morning at 9 a.m.

Among, Between   Use *among* when referring to three or more things and *between* when referring to two things.

> The decision was discussed **among** all the members of the committee.

> I had to decide **between** the chocolate mousse pie and the almond ice cream.

Amount, Number   Use *amount* for things or ideas that are general or abstract and cannot be counted. For example, *furniture* is a general term and cannot be counted. That is, we cannot say *one furniture* or *two furnitures*. Use *number* for things that can be counted (for example, *four chairs* or *three tables*).

> He had a huge **amount** of work to finish before the deadline.

> There were a **number** of people who saw the accident.

An   See the entry for **a, an**.

And   Although some people discourage the use of *and* as the first word in a sentence, it is an acceptable word with which to begin a sentence.

And Etc.   Adding *and* is redundant because *et* means *and* in Latin. See the entry for **etc.**

Anybody, Any Body   See the entry for **anyone, any one**.

Anyone, Any One   *Anyone* means *any person at all*. *Any one* refers to a specific person or thing in a group. There are similar distinctions for other words ending in *–body* and *–one* (for example, *everybody, every body, anybody, any body, some-one,* and *some one*).

The teacher asked if **anyone** knew the answer.

Any one of those children could have taken the ball.

Anyways, Anywheres   These are nonstandard forms for *anyway* and *anywhere*.

As, As If, As Though, Like   Use *as* in a comparison (not *like*) when there is an equality intended or when the meaning is *in the function of*.

Celia acted **as** [not *like*] the leader when the group was getting organized. (Celia = leader)

Use *as if* or *as though* for the subjunctive.

He spent his money **as if** [or **as though**] he were rich.

Use *like* in a comparison (not *as*) when the meaning is *in the manner of* or *to the same degree as*.

The boy swam **like** a fish.

Don't use *like* as the opening word in a clause in formal writing:

Informal: **Like** I thought, he was unable to predict the weather.
Formal: **As** I thought, he was unable to predict the weather.

Assure, Ensure, Insure   *Assure* means *to declare or promise*, *ensure* means *to make safe or certain*, and *insure* means *to protect with a contract of insurance*.

I **assure** you that I am trying to find your lost package.

Some people claim that eating properly **ensures** good health.

This insurance policy also **insures** my car against theft.

Awful, Awfully   *Awful* is an adjective meaning *inspiring awe* or *extremely unpleasant*.

He was involved in an **awful** accident.

Awfully is an adverb used in very informal writing to mean *very*. Avoid it in formal writing.

Informal: The dog was **awfully** dirty.

Awhile, A While *Awhile* is an adverb meaning *a short time* and modifies a verb:

He talked **awhile** and then left.

A while is an article with the noun *while* and means *a period of time*:

I'll be there in **a while**.

Bad, Badly *Bad* is an adjective and is used after linking verbs. *Badly* is an adverb. (See section 15.)

The wheat crop looked **bad** [not *badly*] because of lack of rain.

There was a **bad** flood last summer.

The building was **badly** constructed and unable to withstand the strong winds.

Beside, Besides *Beside* is a preposition meaning *at the side of, compared with*, or *having nothing to do with. Besides* is a preposition meaning *in addition to* or *other than. Besides* as an adverb means *also* or *moreover*. Don't confuse *beside* with *besides*.

That is **beside** the point.

Besides the radio, they had no other means of contact with the outside world.

Besides, I enjoyed the concert.

Between, Among See the entry for **among, between**.

Breath, Breathe *Breath* is a noun, and *breathe* is a verb.

She held her **breath** when she dived into the water.

Learn to **breathe** deeply when you swim.

But Although some people discourage the use of *but* as the first word in a sentence, it is an acceptable word with which to begin a sentence.

Can, May *Can* is a verb that expresses ability, knowledge, or capacity:

He **can** play both the violin and the cello.

May is a verb that expresses possibility or permission. Careful writers avoid using *can* to mean *permission*:

May [not *can*] I sit here?

Can't Hardly   This is incorrect because it is a double negative.

She ~~can't~~ hardly hear normal voice levels. *(can)*

Choose, Chose   *Choose* is the present tense of the verb, and *chose* is the past tense:

Jennie should **choose** strawberry ice cream.

Yesterday, she **chose** strawberry-flavored popcorn.

Cite, Site   *Cite* is a verb that means *to quote an authority or source*; *site* is a noun referring to *a place*.

Be sure to **cite** your sources in the paper.

That is the **site** of the new city swimming pool.

Cloth, Clothe   *Cloth* is a noun, and *clothe* is a verb.

Here is some **cloth** for a new scarf.

His paycheck helps to feed and **clothe** many people in his family.

Compared to, Compared with   Use *compared to* when showing that two things are alike. Use *compared with* when showing similarities and differences.

The speaker **compared** the economy to a roller coaster because both have sudden ups and downs.

The detective **compared** the fingerprints with other sets from a previous crime.

Could of   This is incorrect. Instead use *could have*.

Data   This is the plural form of *datum*. In informal usage, *data* is used as a singular noun, with a singular verb. However, because dictionaries do not accept this, use *data* as a plural form for academic writing.

Informal Usage: The **data** is inconclusive.
Formal Usage: The **data** are inconclusive.

Different from, Different than   *Different from* is always correct, but some writers use *different than* if a clause follows this phrase.

This program is **different from** the others.

That is a **different** result **than** they predicted.

Done   The past tense forms of the verb *do* are *did* and *done*. *Did* is the simple form that needs no additional verb as a helper. *Done* is the past form that requires the helper *have*. Some writers make the mistake of interchanging *did* and *done*.

They ~~done~~ it again. (or) They ~~done~~ it again.

did   *have done*

Effect, Affect   See the entry for **affect, effect**.

Ensure   See the entry for **assure, ensure, insure**.

Etc.   This is an abbreviation of the Latin *et cetera*, meaning *and the rest*. Because it should be used sparingly if at all in formal academic writing, substitute other phrases such as *and so forth* or *and so on*.

Everybody, Every Body   See the entry for **anyone, any one**.

Everyone, Every One   See the entry for **anyone, any one**.

Except, Accept   See the entry for **accept, except**.

Farther, Further   Although some writers use these words interchangeably, dictionary definitions differentiate them. *Farther* is used when actual distance is involved, and *further* is used to mean *to a greater extent, more*.

The house is **farther** from the road than I realized.

That was **furthest** from my thoughts at the time.

Fewer, Less   *Fewer* is used for things that can be counted (*fewer trees, fewer people*), and *less* is used for ideas, abstractions, things that are thought of collectively, not separately (*less trouble, less furniture*), and things that are measured by amount, not number (*less milk, less fuel*).

Fun   This noun is used informally as an adjective.

Informal: They had a **fun** time.

Goes, Says   *Goes* is a nonstandard form of *says*.

Whenever I give him a book to read, he ~~goes~~ "What's it about?"

says

Gone, Went   Past tense forms of the verb *go*. *Went* is the simple form that needs no additional verb as a helper. *Gone* is the past form that requires the helper *have*. Some writers make the mistake of interchanging *went* and *gone*. (See section 13b.)

They ~~gone~~ away yesterday.

went (or) have gone

Good, Well   *Good* is an adjective and therefore describes only nouns. *Well* is an adverb and therefore describes adjectives, other adverbs, and verbs. The word *well* is used as an adjective only in the sense of *in good health*. (See section 15.)

The stereo works ~~good~~ *well*. I feel ~~good~~ *well*.

She is a **good** driver.

Got, Have   *Got* is the past tense of *get* and should not be used in place of *have*. Similarly, *got to* should not be used as a substitute for *must*. *Have got to* is an informal substitute for *must*.

Do you ~~got~~ *have* any pennies for the meter?

I ~~got to~~ *must* go now.

Informal: You **have got to** see that movie.

Great   This adjective is overworked in its formal meaning of *very enjoyable, good*, or *wonderful* and should be reserved for its more exact meanings such as *of remarkable ability, intense, high degree of*, and so on.

Informal: That was a **great** movie.

More exact uses of *great*:

The vaccine was a **great** discovery.

The map went into **great** detail.

Have, Got   See the entry for **got, have**.

Have, Of   *Have*, not *of*, should follow verbs such as *could, might, must*, and *should*.

They should ~~of~~ *have* called by now.

Hisself   This is a nonstandard substitute for *himself*.

Hopefully   This adverb means *in a hopeful way*. Many people consider the meaning *it is to be hoped* as unacceptable.

Acceptable: He listened **hopefully** for the knock at the door.

Often considered
Unacceptable: **Hopefully**, it will not rain tonight.

I   Although some people discourage the use of *I* in formal essays, it is acceptable. If you wish to eliminate the use of *I*, see section 7 on passive verbs.

Imply, Infer   Some writers use these interchangeably, but careful writers maintain the distinction between the two words. *Imply* means *to suggest without stating directly, to hint. Infer* means *to reach an opinion from facts or reasoning.*

The tone of her voice **implied** he was stupid.

The anthropologist **inferred** this was a burial site for prehistoric people.

Insure   See the entry for **assure, ensure, insure**.

Irregardless   This is an incorrect form of the word *regardless*.

Is When, Is Why, Is Where, Is Because   These are incorrect forms for definitions. See section 6 and the Glossary of Grammatical Terms on faulty predication.

Faulty predication: Nervousness is when my palms sweat.
Revised: When I am nervous, my palms sweat.

(or)

Nervousness is a state of being very uneasy or agitated.

Its, It's   *Its* is a personal pronoun in the possessive case. *It's* is a contraction for *it is*.

The kitten licked **its** paw.

It's a good time for a vacation.

Kind, Sort   These two forms are singular and should be used with *this* or *that*. Use *kinds* or *sorts* with *these* or *those*.

This **kind** of cloud indicates heavy rain.

These **sorts** of plants are regarded as weeds.

Lay, Lie   *Lay* is a verb that needs an object and should not be used in place of *lie*, a verb that takes no direct object. (See section 13b.)

He should ~~lay~~ *lie* down and rest awhile.

You can ~~lie~~ *lay* that package on the front table.

Leave, Let   *Leave* means *to go away*, and *let* means *to permit*. It is incorrect to use *leave* when you mean *let*:

~~Leave~~ *Let* me get that for you.

Less, Fewer   See the entry for **fewer, less**.

Let, Leave   See the entry for **leave, let**.

Like, As   See the entry for **as, as if, like**.

Like for   The phrase "I'd like for you to do that" is incorrect. Omit *for*.

May, Can   See the entry for **can, may**.

Most   It is incorrect to use *most* as a substitute for *almost*.

Nowheres   This is an incorrect form of *nowhere*.

Number, Amount   See the entry for **amount, number**.

Of, Have   See the entry for **have, of**.

Off of   It is incorrect to write *off of* for *off* in a phrase such as *off the table*.

O.K., Ok, Okay   These can be used informally but should not be used in formal or academic writing.

Reason . . . Because   This is redundant. Instead of *because*, use *that*:

The reason she dropped the course is ~~because~~ *that* she

couldn't keep up with the homework.

Less wordy revision: She dropped the course **because** she couldn't keep up with the homework.

Reason Why   Using *why* is redundant. Drop the word *why*.

The reason ~~why~~ I called is to remind you of your promise.

Saw, Seen   Past tense forms of the verb *see*. *Saw* is the simple form that needs no additional verb as a helper. *Seen* is the past form that requires the helper *have*. Some writers make the mistake of interchanging *saw* and *seen*. (See section 13b.)

They ~~seen~~ *saw* it happen. (or) They ~~seen~~ *have seen* it happen.

Set, Sit   *Set* means *to place* and is followed by a direct object. *Sit* means *to be seated*. It is incorrect to substitute *set* for *sit*.

Come in and ~~set~~ *sit* down.

~~Sit~~ *Set* the flowers on the table.

Should of   This is incorrect. Instead use *should have*.

Sit, Set   See the entry for **set, sit**.

Site, Cite   See the entry for **cite, site**.

Somebody, Some Body   See the entry for **anyone, any one**.

Someone, Some One   See the entry for **anyone, any one**.

Sort, Kind   See the entry for **kind, sort**.

Such   This is an overworked word when used in place of *very* or *extremely*.

Suppose to, Use to   These are nonstandard forms for *supposed to* and *used to*.

Sure   The use of *sure* as an adverb is informal. Careful writers use *surely* instead.

Informal: I **sure** hope you can join us.
Revised: I **surely** hope you can join us.

Than, Then   *Than* is a conjunction introducing the second element in comparison. *Then* is an adverb meaning *at that time, next, after that, also,* or *in that case.*

She is taller **than** I am.

He picked up the ticket and **then** left the house.

That There, This Here, These Here, Those There   These are incorrect forms for *that, this, these, those.*

That, Which   Use *that* for essential clauses and *which* for nonessential clauses. Some writers, however, also use *which* for essential clauses. (See section 19c.)

Their, There, They're   *Their* is a possessive pronoun; *there* means *in, at,* or *to that place*; and *they're* is a contraction for *they are.*

Their house has been sold.

There is the parking lot.

They're both good swimmers.

Theirself, Theirselves, Themself   These are all incorrect forms for *themselves.*

Them   It is incorrect to use this in place of either the pronoun *these* or *those.*

Look at ~~them~~ those apples.

Then, Than   See the entry for **than, then**.

Thusly   This is an incorrect substitute for *thus.*

To, Too, Two   *To* is a preposition; *too* is an adverb meaning *very* or *also*; and *two* is a number.

He brought his bass guitar **to** the party.

He brought his drums **too**.

He had **two** music stands.

Toward, Towards   Both are accepted forms with the same meaning, although *toward* is preferred in American usage.

Use to   This is incorrect for the modal meaning *formerly*. Instead, use *used to*.

Use to, Suppose to   See the entry for **suppose to, use to**.

Want for   Omit the incorrect *for* in phrases such as "I want *for* you to come here."

Well, Good   See the entry for **good, well**.

Went, Gone   See the entry for **gone, went**.

Where   It is incorrect to use *where* to mean *when* or *that*.

The Fourth of July is a holiday ~~where~~ *when* the town council shoots off fireworks.

I see ~~where~~ *that* there is now a ban on shooting panthers.

Where . . . at   This is a redundant form. Omit *at*.

This is where the picnic is ~~at~~.

Which, That   See the entry for **that, which**.

While, Awhile   See the entry for **awhile, a while**.

Who, Whom   Use *who* for the subjective case; use *whom* for the objective case.

He is the person **who** signs that form.

He is the person **whom** I asked for help.

Who's, Whose   *Who's* is a contraction for *who is*; *whose* is a possessive pronoun.

Who's included on that list?

Whose wristwatch is this?

Your, You're   *Your* is a possessive pronoun; *you're* is a contraction for *you are*.

Your hands are cold.

You're a great success.

Glossary of Grammatical Terms

Absolutes Words or phrases that modify whole sentences rather than parts of sentences or individual words. An absolute phrase, which consists of a noun and participle, can be placed anywhere in the sentence but needs to be set off from the sentence by commas.

> **The snow having finally stopped,** the football
> *(absolute phrase)*
>
> game began.

Abstract Nouns Nouns that refer to ideas, qualities, generalized concepts, and conditions and do not have plural forms. (See section 31.)

> happiness, pride, furniture, trouble, sincerity

Active Voice See **Voice**.

Adjective Clauses See **Dependent Clauses**.

Adjectives Words that modify nouns and pronouns. (See section 15.)

Descriptive adjectives (*red, clean, beautiful, offensive,* for example) have three forms:

Positive:	red, clean, beautiful, offensive
Comparative	(for comparing two things): cleaner, more beautiful, less offensive
Superlative	(for comparing more than two things): cleanest, most beautiful, least offensive

Adverb Clauses See **Dependent Clauses**.

Adverbs Modify verbs, verb forms, adjectives, and other adverbs. (See section 15.) Descriptive adverbs (for example, *fast, graceful, awkward*) have three forms:

266

Positive: fast, graceful, awkward

Comparative   (for comparing two things): faster, more
                 graceful, less awkward

Superlative   (for comparing more than two things): fastest,
                 most graceful, least awkward

Agreement   The use of the corresponding form for related words in order to have them agree in number, person, or gender. (See sections 13a and 14b.)

John runs. (Both subject and verb are singular.)

It is necessary to flush the **pipes** regularly so that **they** don't freeze.

(Both subjects, it *and* they, *are in third person;* they *agrees in number with the antecedent,* pipes.*)*

Antecedents   Words or groups of words to which pronouns refer.

When the **bell** was rung, **it** sounded very loudly.

(Bell is the antecedent of *it.)*

Antonyms   Words with opposite meanings.

Word	Antonym
hot	cold
fast	slow
noisy	quiet

Appositives   Nonessential phrases and clauses that follow nouns and identify or explain them. (See section 19c.)

My uncle, **who lives in Wyoming**, is taking windsurfing
             (appositive)

lessons in Florida.

Articles   See **Noun Determiners** and section 32.

Auxiliary Verbs   Verbs used with main verbs in verb phrases.

should be going   **has** taken
(auxiliary verb)   (auxiliary verb)

Cardinal Numbers   See **Noun Determiners**.

Case   The form or position of a noun or pronoun that shows its use or relationship to other words in a sentence. The three cases in English are (1) subject (or subjective or nominative), (2) object (or objective), and (3) possessive (or genitive). (See section 14a.)

Clauses   Groups of related words that contain both subjects and predicates and function either as sentences or as parts of sentences. Clauses are either independent (or main) or dependent (or subordinate). (See section 11.)

Collective Nouns   Nouns that refer to groups of people or things, such as a *committee, team,* or *jury*. When the group includes a number of members acting as a unit and is the subject of the sentence, the verb is also singular. (See section 13a.)

The **jury** has made a decision.

Comma Splices   Punctuation errors in which two or more independent clauses in compound sentences are separated only by commas and no coordinating conjunctions. (See section 12.)

Jessie said he could not help, *but (or) ;*

that was typical of his responses to requests.

Common Nouns   Nouns that refer to general rather than specific categories of people, places, and things and are not capitalized. (See section 24a.)

basket, person, history, tractor

Comparative   The form of adjectives and adverbs used when two things are being compared. (See section 15.)

higher, more intelligent, less friendly

Complement   When linking verbs link subjects to adjectives or nouns, the adjectives or nouns are complements.

Phyllis was **tired**.
        (complement)

She became a **musician**.
            (complement)

Complex Sentences   Sentences with at least one independent clause and at least one dependent clause arranged in any order.

Compound-Complex Sentences   Sentences with at least two independent clauses and at least one dependent clause arranged in any order.

Compound Nouns   Words such as *swimming pool, dropout, roommate*, and *stepmother*, in which more than one word is needed.

Compound Sentences   Sentences with two or more independent clauses and no dependent clauses. (See section 12.)

Conjunctions   Words that connect other words, phrases, and clauses in sentences. *Coordinating conjunctions* connect independent clauses; *subordinating conjunctions* connect dependent or subordinating clauses with independent or main clauses.

Coordinating: and, but, for, or, nor, so, yet
Conjunctions: until, while
Some Subordinating Conjunctions: after, although, because, if, since

Conjunctive Adverbs   Words that begin or join independent clauses. (See section 19a.)

consequently, however, therefore, thus, moreover

Connotation   The attitudes and emotional overtones beyond the direct definition of a word.

The words *plump* and *fat* both mean *fleshy*, but *plump* has a more positive connotation than *fat*.

Consistency   Maintaining the same voice with pronouns, the same tense with verbs, and the same tone, voice, or mode of discourse. (See section 17.)

Coordinating Conjunctions   See **Conjunctions**.

Coordination   Of equal importance. Two independent clauses in the same sentence are coordinate because they have equal importance and the same emphasis.

Correlative Conjunctions   Words that work in pairs and give emphasis.

both . . . and   neither . . . nor   either . . . or

not . . . but also

Dangling Modifiers   Phrases or clauses in which the doer of the action is not clearly indicated. (See section 16a.)

Tim thought

Missing an opportunity to study,

^

the exam seemed especially difficult.

Declarative Mood   See **Mood**.

Demonstrative Pronouns   Pronouns that refer to things. (See **Noun Determiners**.)

this, that, these, those

Denotation   The explicit dictionary definition of a word, as opposed to the connotation of a word. (See **Connotation**.)

Dependent Clauses (Subordinate Clauses)   Clauses that cannot stand alone as complete sentences. (See section 11.) There are two kinds of dependent clauses: adverb clauses and adjective clauses.

Adverb clauses:	Begin with subordinating conjunctions such as *after, if, because, while, when.*
Adjective clauses:	Tell more about nouns or pronouns in sentences and begin with words such as *who, which, that, whose, whom.*

Determiner   See **Noun Determiner**.

Diagrams   See **Sentence Diagrams**.

Direct Discourse   See **Mode of Discourse**.

Direct/Indirect Quotations   Direct quotations are the exact words said by someone or the exact words in print that are being copied. Indirect quotations are not the exact words but the rephrasing or summarizing of someone else's words. (See section 22a.)

Direct Objects   Nouns or pronouns that follow a transitive verb and complete the meaning or receive the action of the verb. The direct object answers the question *what?* or *whom?*

Ellipsis   A series of three dots to indicate that words or parts of sentences are being omitted from material being quoted. (See section 23.)

Essential and Nonessential Clauses and Phrases
Essential (also called restrictive) clauses and phrases appear after nouns and are necessary or essential to complete the meaning of the sentence. **Nonessential** (also called nonrestrictive) clauses and phrases appear after nouns and add extra information, but that information can be removed from the sentence without altering the meaning. (See section 19c.)

Apples **that are green** are not sweet.
(essential clause)

Golden Delicious apples, **which are yellow**, are sweet.
(nonessential clause)

Excessive Coordination   Occurs when too many equal clauses are strung together with coordinators into one sentence.

Excessive Subordination   Occurs when too many subordinate clauses are strung together in a complex sentence.

Faulty Coordination   Occurs when two clauses that are either unequal in importance or that have little or no connection to each other are combined in one sentence and written as independent clauses.

Faulty Parallelism   See **Parallel Construction**.

Faulty Predication Occurs when a predicate does not appropriately fit the subject. This happens most often after forms of the *to be* verb. (See section 6.)

He

~~The reason he~~ was late was

^

because he had to study.

Fragments Groups of words punctuated as sentences that either do not have both a subject and a complete verb or that are dependent clauses. (See section 11.)

Whenever we wanted to pick fresh fruit while we were

, we would head for the orchard with buckets

staying on my grandmother's farm ^.

Fused Sentences Punctuation errors (also called *run-ons*) in which there is no punctuation between independent clauses in the sentence. (See section 12.)

;

Jennifer never learned how to ask politely

^

she just took what she wanted.

Gerunds Verbal forms ending in *–ing* that function as nouns. (See **Phrases** and **Verbals**.)

Arnon enjoys **cooking**.

(gerund)

Jogging is another of his pastimes.

(gerund)

Homonyms Words that sound alike but are spelled differently and have different meanings. (See section 28b.)

hear/here   passed/past   buy/by

Idioms Expressions meaning something beyond the simple definition or literal translation into another language. For example, idioms such as "short and sweet" or "wearing his heart on his sleeve" are expressions in English that cannot be translated literally into another language. (See section 35.)

Imperative Mood See **Mood**.

Indefinite Pronouns Pronouns that make indefinite reference to nouns.

anyone, everyone, nobody, something

Independent Clauses Clauses that can stand alone as complete sentences because they do not depend on other clauses to complete their meanings. (See section 11.)

Indirect Discourse   See **Mode of Discourse**.

Indirect Objects   Words that follow transitive verbs and come before direct objects. They indicate the one to whom or for whom something is given, said, or done and answer the questions to *what?* or to *whom?* Indirect objects can always be paraphrased by a prepositional phrase beginning with *to* or *for*.

   Alice gave **me** some money.
     (indirect object)

Paraphrase: Alice gave some money to me.

Infinitives   Phrases made up of the present form of the verb preceded by *to*. Infinitives can have subjects, objects, complements, or modifiers. (See section 16c.)

   Everyone wanted **to swim** in the new pool.
                  (infinitive)

Intensifiers   Modifying words used for emphasis.

   She **most certainly** did fix that car!
        (intensifiers)

Interjections   Words used as exclamations.

   Oh, I don't think I want to know about that.
   (interjection)

Interrogative Pronouns   Pronouns used in questions.

   who, whose, whom, which, that

Intransitive Verbs   See **Verbs**.

Irregular Verbs   Verbs in which the past tense forms and/or the past participles are not formed by adding *–ed* or *–d*. (See section 13b.)

   do, did, done   begin, began, begun

Jargon   Words and phrases that are either the specialized language of various fields or, in a negative sense, unnecessarily technical or inflated terms. (See section 5.)

Linking Verbs   Verbs linking the subject to the subject complement. The most common linking verbs are *appear, seem, become, feel, look, taste, sound*, and *be*.

   I **feel** sleepy. He **became** the president.
   (linking verb)   (linking verb)

Misplaced Modifiers   Modifiers not placed next to or close to the word(s) being modified. (See section 16a.)

                        on television
   We saw an advertisement for an excellent new stereo
                      ^
   system with dual headphones ~~on television~~.

Modal Verbs   Helping verbs such as *shall, should, will, would, can, could, may, might, must, ought to,* and *used to* that express an attitude such as interest, possibility, or obligation. (See section 30b.)

Mode of Discourse   Direct discourse repeats the exact words that someone says, and indirect discourse reports the words but changes some of the words.

> Everett said, **"I want to become a physicist."**
>
> *(direct discourse)*

> Everett said **that he wants to become a physicist**.
>
> *(indirect discourse)*

Modifiers   Words or groups of words that describe or limit other words, phrases, and clauses. The most common modifiers are adjectives and adverbs. (See section 16.)

Mood   Verbs indicate whether a sentence expresses a fact (the declarative or indicative mood); expresses some doubt or something contrary to fact or states a recommendation (the subjunctive mood); or issues a command (the imperative mood).

Nonessential Clauses and Phrases   See **Essential and Nonessential Clauses and Phrases**.

Nonrestrictive Clauses and Phrases   See **Essential and Nonessential Clauses and Phrases**.

Noun Clauses   Subordinate clauses used as nouns.

> **What I see here** is adequate.
>
> *(noun clause)*

Noun Determiners   Words that signal a noun is about to follow. They stand next to their nouns or can be separated by adjectives. Some noun determiners can also function as nouns. There are five types of noun determiners:

1. Articles: definite: *the*; indefinite: *a, an*

2. Demonstratives: *this, that, these, those*

3. Possessives: *my, our, your, his, her, its, their*

4. Cardinal numbers: *one, two, three,* and so on

5. Miscellaneous: *all, another, each, every, much,* and *others*

Noun Phrases   See **Phrases**.

Nouns   Words that name people, places, things, and ideas and have plural or possessive endings. Nouns function as subjects, direct objects, predicate nominatives, objects of prepositions, and indirect objects.

Number   The quantity expressed by a noun or pronoun, either singular (one) or plural (more than one).

Object Complements   The adjectives in predicates modifying the object of the verb (not the subject).

The enlargement makes the picture **clear**.
              (object complement)

Objective Case of Pronouns   The case needed when the pronoun is the direct or indirect object of the verb or the object of a preposition.

Singular

First person: *me*
Second person: *you*
Third person: *him, her, it*

Plural

First person: *us*
Second person: *you*
Third person: *them*

Object of the Preposition   Noun following the preposition. The preposition, its object, and any modifiers make up the prepositional phrase.

For **Daniel**
(object of the preposition for)

She knocked twice **on the big wooden door**.
              (prepositional phrase)

Objects   See **Direct Objects** and **Object Complements**.

Parallel Construction   When two or more items are listed or compared, they must be in the same grammatical form as equal elements. When items are not in the same grammatical form, they lack parallel structure (often called *faulty parallelism*). (See section 8.)

She was sure that **being an apprentice in a photographer's studio** would be more useful than **being a student in photography classes**.

(The phrases in bold type are parallel because they have the same grammatical form.)

Parenthetical Elements   Nonessential words, phrases, and clauses set off by commas, dashes, or parentheses.

Participles   Verb forms that may be part of the complete verb or function as adjectives or adverbs. The present participle ends in *–ing*, and the past participle usually ends in *–ed, –d, –n,* or *–t*. (See **Phrases**.)

Present participles: *running, sleeping, digging*

She is **running** for mayor in this campaign.
      (present participle)

Past participles: *walked, deleted, chosen*

The **elected** candidate will take office in January.
     (past participle)

Parts of Speech   The eight classes into which words are grouped according to their function, place, meaning, and use in a sentence: nouns, pronouns, verbs, adjectives, adverbs, prepositions, conjunctions, and interjections.

Passive Voice   See **Voice**.

Past Participle   See **Participles**.

Perfect Progressive Tense   See **Verb Tenses**.

Perfect Tenses   See **Verb Tenses**.

Person   There are three "persons" in English.

First person: the person(s) speaking

   I or *we*

Second person: the person(s) spoken to

   you

Third person: the person(s) spoken about

   he, she, it, they, anyone, etc.

Personal Pronouns   Refer to people or things.

	Subject	Object	Possessive
Singular			
First person	I	me	my, mine
Second person	you	you	your, yours
Third person	he, she, it	him, her, it	his, her, hers, its
Plural			
First person	we	us	our, ours
Second person	you	you	your, yours
Third person	they	them	their, theirs

Phrases   Groups of related words without subjects and predicates.

Verb phrases function as verbs.

   She **has been eating** too much sugar.
      (verb phrase)

Noun phrases function as nouns.

   A major winter storm hit **the eastern coast of Maine**.
      (noun phrase)   *(noun phrase)*

Prepositional phrases usually function as modifiers.

   That book **of hers** is overdue at the library.
      (prepositional phrase)

Participial phrases, gerund phrases, infinitive phrases, appositive phrases, and absolute phrases function as adjectives, adverbs, or nouns.

Participial Phrase:	I saw people **staring at my peculiar-looking haircut**.
Gerund Phrase:	**Making copies of videotapes** can be illegal.
Infinitive Phrase:	He likes **to give expensive presents**.
Appositive Phrase:	You ought to see Dr. Elman, **a dermatologist**.
Absolute Phrase:	**The test done**, he sighed with relief.

Possessive Pronouns See **Personal Pronouns, Noun Determiners**, and section 14a.

Predicate Adjectives See **Subject Complements**.

Predicate Nominatives See **Subject Complements**.

Predication Words or groups of words that express action or state of beginning in a sentence and consist of one or more verbs, plus any complements or modifiers.

Prefixes Word parts added to the beginning of words.

Prefix	**Word**
bio– (life)	biography
mis– (wrong, bad)	misspell

Prepositions Link and relate their objects (usually nouns or pronouns) to some other word or words in a sentence. Prepositions usually precede their objects but may follow the objects and appear at the end of the sentence.

The server gave the check **to my date** by mistake.
(prepositional phrase)

I wonder **what** she is asking **for**.
(object of the preposition)　　(preposition)

Prepositional Phrases See **Phrases**.

Progressive Tenses See **Verb Tenses**.

Pronouns Words that substitute for nouns. (See section 14.) Pronouns should refer to previously stated nouns, called antecedents.

When **Josh** came in, **he** brought some firewood.
(antecedent)　　(pronoun)

Forms of pronouns: personal, possessive, reflexive, interrogative, demonstrative, indefinite, and relative.

Pronoun Case   Refers to the form of the pronoun that is needed in a sentence. See **Subjective, Objective**, and **Possessive Cases** and section 14a.

Proper Nouns   Refer to specific people, places, and things. Proper nouns are always capitalized. (See section 24a.)

Copenhagen   Honda   House of Representatives   Spanish

Reflexive Pronouns   Pronouns that show someone or something in the sentence is acting for itself or on itself. Because a reflexive pronoun must refer to a word in a sentence, it is not the subject or direct object. If used to show emphasis, reflexive pronouns are called intensive pronouns. (See section 14a.)

Singular	Plural
First person: *myself*	First person: *ourselves*
Second person: *yourself*	Second person: *yourselves*
Third person: *himself,*	Third person: *themselves*
herself, itself	

She returned the book **herself** rather than giving it to
(reflexive pronoun)

her roommate to bring back.

Relative Pronouns   Pronouns that show the relationship of a dependent clause to a noun in the sentence. Relative pronouns substitute for nouns already mentioned in sentences and introduce adjective or noun clauses and include *that, which, who, whom,* and *whose.*

This was the movie **that** won the Academy Award.

Restrictive Clauses and Phrases   See **Essential and Nonessential Clauses and Phrases**.

Run-on Sentences   See **Fused Sentences** and section 12.

Sentences   Groups of words that have at least one independent clause (a complete unit of thought with a subject and predicate). Sentences can be classified by their structure as simple, compound, complex, and compound-complex.

Simple:	one independent clause
Compound:	two or more independent clauses
Complex:	one or more independent clauses and one or more dependent clauses

Compound-complex: two or more independent clauses and one or more dependent clauses

Sentences can also be classified by their function as declarative, interrogative, imperative, and exclamatory.

Declarative: makes a statement
Interrogative: asks a question
Imperative: issues a command
Exclamatory: makes an exclamation

Sentence Diagrams   A method of showing relationships within a sentence.

> Marnie's **cousin**, who has no taste in food, **ordered** a **hamburger** with coleslaw at the Chinese restaurant.

Sentence Fragment   See **Fragment**.

Simple Sentence   See **Sentence**.

Simple Tenses   See **Verb Tenses**.

Split Infinitives   Phrases in which modifiers are inserted between to and the verb. Some people object to split infinitives, but others consider them grammatically acceptable.

> to quickly turn   to easily reach   to forcefully enter

Subject   The word or words in a sentence that act or are acted upon by the verb or are linked by the verb to another word or words in the sentence. The *simple subject* includes only the noun or other main word or words, and the *complete subject* includes all the modifiers with the subject.

> **Harvey** objected to his roommate's alarm going off at 9 A.M.
>
> (Harvey is the subject.)
>
> **Every single one of the people in the room** heard her giggle.
>
> (The simple subject is one; the complete subject is the whole phrase.)

Subjective Case of Pronouns   See **Personal Pronouns** and section 14.

Subject Complement   The noun or adjective in the predicate (predicate noun or adjective) that refers to the same entity as the subject in sentences with linking verbs, such as *is/are, feel, look, smell, sound, taste*, and *seem*.

She feels **happy**.

   (subject complement)

He is a **pharmacist**.

   (subject complement)

Subjunctive Mood   See **Mood**.

Subordinating Conjunctions   Words such as *although, if, until*, and *when*, that join two clauses and subordinate one to the other.

She is late. She overslept.

She is late **because** she overslept.

Subordination   The act of placing one clause in a subordinate or dependent relationship to another in a sentence because it is less important and is dependent for its meaning on the other clause.

Suffix   Word part added to the end of a word.

Suffix	Word
–ful	careful
–less	nameless

Superlative Forms of Adjectives and Adverbs   See **Adjectives and Adverbs** and section 15.

Synonyms   Words with similar meanings.

Word	Synonym
damp	moist
pretty	attractive

Tense   See **Verb Tense**.

Tone   The attitude or level of formality reflected in the word choices in a piece of writing. (See section 5.)

Transitions   Words in sentences that show relationships between sentences and paragraphs. (See section 9.)

Transitive Verbs   See **Verbs**.

Verbals   Words that are derived from verbs but do not act as verbs in sentences. Three types of verbals are infinitives, participles, and gerunds.

Infinitives	**to + verb**
to wind	to say

Participles: Words used as modifiers or with helping
                   verbs. The present participle ends in *–ing*,
                   and many past participles end in *—ed*.

   The dog is **panting**.
           (present participle)

   He bought only **used** clothing.
                   (past participle)

Gerunds: Present participles used as nouns.

   Smiling was not a natural act for her.
   (gerund)

Verbs   Words or groups of words (verb phrases) in predicates that express action, show a state of being, or act as a
link between the subject and the rest of the predicate. Verbs
change form to show time (tense), mood, and voice and are
classified as transitive, intransitive, and linking verbs. (See
section 30.)

Transitive verbs: Require objects to complete the
                        predicate.

   He **cut** the cardboard **box** with his knife.
   (transitive verb)   *(object)*

Intransitive verbs: Do not require objects.

   My ancient cat often **lies** on the porch.
                         (intransitive verb)

Linking verbs: Link the subject to the following
                     noun or adjective.

   The trees **are** bare.
             (linking verb)

Verb Conjugations   The forms of verbs in various tenses.
(See section 30a.)

Regular:

Present

Simple present:

I walk	we walk
you walk	you walk
he, she, it walks	they walk

Present progressive:

I am walking	we are walking
you are walking	you are walking
he, she, it is walking	they are walking

Present perfect:

I have walked	we have walked
you have walked	you have walked
he, she, it has walked	they have walked

Present perfect progressive:

I have been walking	we have been walking
you have been walking	you have been walking
he, she, it has been walking	they have been walking

Past

Simple past:

I walked	we walked
you walked	you walked
he, she, it walked	they walked

Past progressive:

I was walking	we were walking
you were walking	you were walking
he, she, it was walking	they were walking

Past perfect:

I had walked	we had walked
you had walked	you had walked
he, she, it had walked	they had walked

Past perfect progressive:

I had been walking	we had been walking
you had been walking	you had been walking
he, she, it had been walking	they had been walking

Future

Simple future:

I shall walk	we shall walk
you will walk	you will walk
he, she, it will walk	they will walk

Future progressive:

I shall be walking	we shall be walking
you will be walking	you will be walking
he, she, it will be walking	they will be walking

Future perfect:

I shall have walked	we shall have walked
you will have walked	you will have walked
he, she, it will have walked	they will have walked

Future perfect progressive:

I shall have been walking	we shall have been walking
you will have been walking	you will have been walking
he, she, it will have been walking	they will have been walking

Irregular:

Present

Simple present:

I go	we go
you go	you go
he, she, it goes	they go

Present progressive:

I am going	we are going
you are going	you are going
he, she, it is going	they are going

Present perfect:

I have gone	we have gone
you have gone	you have gone
he, she, it has gone	they have gone

Present perfect progressive:

I have been going	we have been going
you have been going	you have been going
he, she, it has been going	they have been going

Past

Simple past:

I went	we went
you went	you went
he, she, it went	they went

Past progressive:

I was going	we were going
you were going	you were going
he, she, it was going	they were going

Past perfect:

I had gone	we had gone
you had gone	you had gone
he, she, it had gone	they had gone

Past perfect progressive:

I had been going	we had been going
you had been going	you had been going
he, she, it had been going	they had been going

Future

Simple:

I shall go	we shall go
you will go	you will go
he, she, it will go	they will go

Future progressive:

I shall be going	we shall be going
you will be going	you will be going
he, she, it will be going	they will be going

Future perfect:

I shall have gone	we shall have gone
you will have gone	you will have gone
he, she, it will have gone	they will have gone

Future perfect progressive:

I shall have been going	we shall have been going
you will have been going	you will have been going
he, she, it will have been going	they will have been going

Verb Phrases   See **Verbs**.

Verb Tenses   The times indicated by the verb forms in the past, present, or future. (For the verb forms, see **Verb Conjugations** and section 30a.)

Present

Simple present:
Describes actions or situations that exist now and are habitually or generally true.

I **walk** to class every afternoon.

Present progressive:
Indicates activity in progress, something not finished, or something continuing.

He **is studying** Swedish.

Present perfect:
Describes single or repeated actions that began in the past and lead up to and include the present.

She **has lived** in Alaska for two years.

Present perfect progressive:
Indicates action that began in the past, continues to the present, and may continue into the future.

They **have been building** that garage for six months.

Past

Simple past:
Describes completed actions or conditions in the past.

They **ate** breakfast in the cafeteria.

Past progressive:
Indicates past action that took place over a period of time.

He **was swimming** when the storm began.

Past perfect:
Indicates an action or event was completed before another event in the past.

No one **had heard** about the crisis when the newscast began.

Past perfect progressive:
Indicates an ongoing condition in the past that has ended.

I **had been planning** my trip to Mexico when I heard about the earthquake.

Future

Simple future:
Indicates actions or events in the future.

The store **will open** at 9 A.M.

Future progressive:
Indicates future action that will continue for some time.

I **will be working** on that project next week.

Future perfect:
Indicates action that will be completed by or before a specified time in the future.

Next summer, they **will have been** here for twenty years.

Future perfect progressive:
Indicates ongoing actions or conditions until a specific time in the future.

By tomorrow, I **will have been waiting** for the delivery for one month.

Voice   Verbs are either in the *active* or *passive* voice. In the active voice, the subject performs the action of the verb. In the passive, the subject receives the action. (See section 7.)

The dog **bit** the boy.
  (active verb)

The boy **was bitten** by the dog.
  (passive verb)

Index